BEST ROAD TRIPS
ONTARIO &
QUÉBEC

- - - - - - - →

ESCAPES ON THE OPEN ROAD

T0003179

Shawn Duthie
Steve Fallon, Carolyn Heller
Liza Prado, Phillip Tang

SYMBOLS IN THIS BOOK

✓ Top Tips

📖 History & Culture

📷 Essential Photo

🔗 Link Your Trips

👫 Family

🏃 Walking Tour

💬 Tips from Locals

🍷 Food & Drink

✗ Eating

↱ Trip Detour

🌳 Outdoors

🛏 Sleeping

☏ Telephone Number

@ Internet Access

📖 English-Language Menu

🕐 Opening Hours

📶 Wi-Fi Access

👪 Family-Friendly

🅿 Parking

✎ Vegetarian Selection

🐾 Pet-Friendly

🚭 Nonsmoking

🏊 Swimming Pool

❄ Air-Conditioning

MAP LEGEND

Routes

▬▬ Trip Route
▬▬ Trip Detour
▬▬ Linked Trip
▬▬ Walk Route
▬▬ Tollway
▬▬ Freeway
▬▬ Primary
▬▬ Secondary
▬▬ Tertiary
Lane
Unsealed Road
Plaza/Mall
Steps
)═(Tunnel
Pedestrian Overpass
--- Walk Track/Path

Trips

1 Trip Numbers
9 Trip Stop
🏃 Walking tour
↱ Trip Detour

Population

◎ Capital (National)
◉ Capital (State/Province)
● City/Large Town
○ Town/Village

Boundaries

--- International
---- State/Province
⌐⌐⌐ Cliff

Hydrography

River/Creek
Swamp/Mangrove
Canal
Water
Dry/Salt/ Intermittent Lake
Glacier

Areas

Beach
Cemetery (Christian)
Cemetery (Other)
Park
Forest
Reservation
Urban Area
Sportsground

Transport

✈ Airport
🚡 Cable Car/ Funicular
Ⓜ Metro/Muni station
Ⓟ Parking
Ⓢ Subway station
Train/Railway
Tram

Route Markers

Ⓣ Trans-Canada Hwy
㉓ Provincial/ Territorial Hwy
㊽ US National Hwy
Ⓓ US Interstate Hwy
㊹ US State Hwy

Note: Not all symbols displayed above appear on the maps in this book

PLAN YOUR TRIP

ROAD TRIPS

DESTINATIONS

CONTENTS

ROAD TRIP ESSENTIALS.... 110

TERRITORY ACKNOWLEDGEMENT

Lonely Planet would like to acknowledge and pay respect to the Indigenous people throughout this country. This guide was written on and is written about land which includes their traditional lands, unceded territories and Treaty territories. We also recognise the ongoing efforts of Indigenous peoples for reconciliation, justice, and social, cultural, and economic self-determination. We hope you can use the opportunity of your travels to connect with the people and learn about Indigenous culture and society.

Le Château Frontenac (p98), Québec City

COVID-19

We have re-checked every business in this book before publication to ensure that it is still open after the COVID-19 outbreak. However, the economic and social impacts of COVID-19 will continue to be felt long after the outbreak has been contained, and many businesses, services and events referenced in this guide may experience ongoing restrictions. Some businesses may be temporarily closed, have changed their opening hours and services, or require bookings; some unfortunately could have closed permanently. We suggest you check with venues before visiting for the latest information.

WELCOME TO
ONTARIO & QUÉBEC

These heavyweight provinces have long been central to Canada's story. More than 60% of the country's population lives here, concentrated in the sophisticated metropolises of Toronto, Ottawa, Montréal and Québec City, yet regions of remarkable beauty and sweeping wilderness areas lie within easy reach.

Ontario's Great Lakes are huge, like inland seas, and boast stunning shoreline drives, with forested reserves and sandy beaches, plus the astonishing Niagara Falls. Cosmopolitan Toronto offers hopping arts and entertainment scenes, kept current by the neighborly influences of New York.

Francophone Montréal and Québec City offer a perfect mix of refinement and playfulness, and history-soaked city quarters. Head to the Eastern Townships and up the Lawrence River for a taste of rustic Québec culture.

And don't miss the region's world-class outdoor activities. So pack your hiking boots and your dancing shoes, and prepare to explore.

Killarney Lake, Killarney Provincial Park (p29)

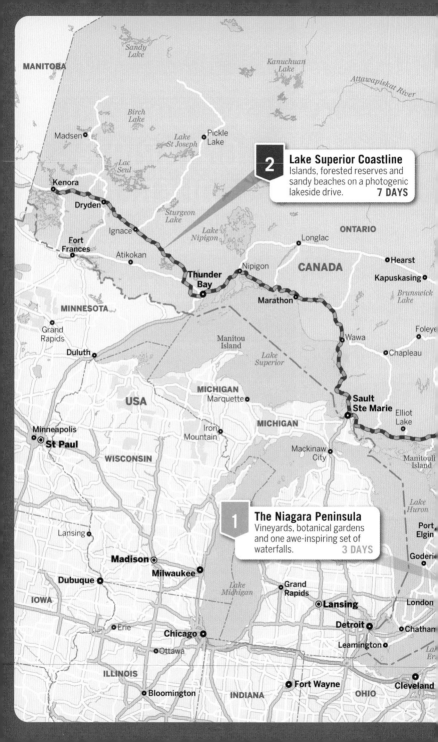

MANITOBA

Sandy
Lake

Kanuchuan
Lake

Attawapiskat River

Madsen

Pickle
Lake

Lake
St Joseph

Birch
Lake

Lac
Seul

2 **Lake Superior Coastline**
Islands, forested reserves and
sandy beaches on a photogenic
lakeside drive. **7 DAYS**

Kenora

Dryden

Sturgeon
Lake

Ignace

Lake
Nipigon

ONTARIO

Longlac

Fort
Frances

Atikokan

Nipigon

CANADA

Hearst

Kapuskasing

**Thunder
Bay**

Marathon

Brunswick
Lake

MINNESOTA

Grand
Rapids

Manitou
Island

Wawa

Foleye

Duluth

Lake
Superior

Chapleau

USA

MICHIGAN
Marquette

**Sault
Ste Marie**

Elliot
Lake

Minneapolis

St Paul

WISCONSIN

Iron
Mountain

MICHIGAN

Mackinaw
City

Manitouli
Island

Lansing

Mackinaw
City

Lake
Huron

1 **The Niagara Peninsula**
Vineyards, botanical gardens
and one awe-inspiring set of
waterfalls. **3 DAYS**

Port
Elgin

Madison

Milwaukee

Goderi

Dubuque

Lake
Michigan

Grand
Rapids

London

IOWA

Lansing

Erie

Chicago

Detroit

Chatha

Ottawa

Leamington

ILLINOIS

Bloomington

INDIANA

Fort Wayne

OHIO

Cleveland

La
Er

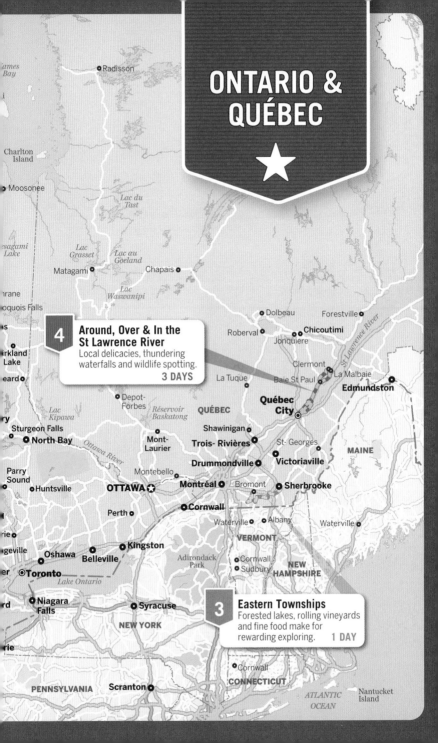

ONTARIO & QUÉBEC

★

4 **Around, Over & In the St Lawrence River**
Local delicacies, thundering waterfalls and wildlife spotting. **3 DAYS**

3 **Eastern Townships**
Forested lakes, rolling vineyards and fine food make for rewarding exploring. **1 DAY**

James Bay

Radisson

Charlton Island

Moosonee

Lac du Tast

sagami Lake

Lac Grasset

Lac au Goeland

Matagami

Chapais

Lac Waswanipi

hrane

oquois Falls

as

irkland Lake

eard

Dolbeau

Forestville

Roberval

Chicoutimi

Jonquiere

Clermont

La Malbaie

La Tuque

Baie St Paul

Edmundston

Depot-Forbes

Réservoir Baskatong

QUÉBEC

Québec City

Lac Kipawa

Mont-Laurier

Shawinigan

St-Georges

ry

Sturgeon Falls

North Bay

Ottawa River

Trois-Rivières

St- Georges

MAINE

Parry Sound

Huntsville

Montebello

Drummondville

Victoriaville

OTTAWA

Montréal

Bromont

Sherbrooke

Perth

Cornwall

Waterville

Albany

Waterville

VERMONT

rie

geville

Oshawa

Belleville

Kingston

Adirondack Park

Cornwall

NEW HAMPSHIRE

er

Toronto

Lake Ontario

Sudbury

Niagara Falls

Syracuse

NEW YORK

Cornwall

rie

PENNSYLVANIA

Scranton

CONNECTICUT

ATLANTIC OCEAN

Nantucket Island

ONTARIO & QUÉBEC

HIGHLIGHTS

★

Niagara Falls (left) North America's highest-volume cascades are mind-blowing, whether experienced by foot, catamaran or chopper flight. See it on Trip **1**

Lake Superior Provincial Park (above) Stunning scenery, gorgeous forests and rock pictographs await you at this most scenic of shoreline parks. See it on Trip **2**

Île d'Orléans (right) Foodies rejoice: the culinary artisans of 'Orléans Island' are just waiting to show off their skills to you. See it on Trip **4**

CITY GUIDE

Old Montréal (p84) Cobblestone streets

MONTRÉAL

North America's largest Francophone city is a blend of French-inspired joie de vivre and cosmopolitan dynamism that has come together to foster a flourishing arts scene, an indie-rock explosion, the Plateau's extraordinary cache of swank eateries and a cool Parisian vibe that pervades every *terrasse* (patio) in the Quartier Latin.

Getting Around

Montréal's four metro lines provide speedy, efficient service around the city and run from 5am to midnight and until 1:30am on Friday and Saturday nights. The city's popular Bixi bike-sharing system has more than 500 stations around town.

Parking

Street parking in Montréal can run to $4 per hour, while overnight lots charge from $17 to $28 for 24 hours. The lot near Longueuil metro station has better prices (from $8.25 for 24 hours).

Where to Eat

Downtown and Plateau Mont-Royal are a diner's delight, linked by arteries Blvd St-Laurent and Rue St-Denis. Mile End and Outremont have a wide selection of bistros and ethnic eateries, particularly along Ave Laurier, Ave St-Viateur and Rue Bernard.

Where to Stay

Old Montréal is ultra-convenient for many sights, old-world charm and access to Old Port. Nearby downtown is handy for key sights and museums. The atmospheric Plateau Mont-Royal has charming B&Bs within strolling distance of great dining and nightlife.

Useful Websites

MTL Blog (www.mtlblog.com) Opinionated local voices on the latest in dining, drinking, festivals and daily life in the city.

Tourisme Montréal (www.mtl.org) Useful multilingual info, travel ideas and events calendar from the city's modern official website.

Trips Through Montréal 3

Toronto (p56) City skyline at twilight

TORONTO

A hyperactive stew of cultures and neighborhoods, Toronto strikes you with sheer urban awe. Will you have dinner in Chinatown or Greektown? Five-star fusion or a peameal bacon sandwich? In Ontario's cool capital, modern-art galleries, theater par excellence, rockin' band rooms and hockey mania add to the megalopolis.

Getting Around

Toronto's subway is the fastest way to get across town; service runs from 6am (8am Sunday) until 1:30am daily.

Parking

Parking in Toronto is expensive, usually $3 to $4 per half hour in a private lot; public lots and street parking range from $1.50 to $4 per hour, depending on the neighborhood. Private lots offer reduced-rate parking before 7am and after 6pm.

Where to Eat

The Financial and Entertainment Districts have fine dining and celebrity chefs, while Kensington Market and Chinatown are all about hole-in-the-wall eats and homegrown talent.

Where to Stay

Downtown puts you in the heart of the action, with a good range of lodging for all budgets and easy subway access. For something more atmospheric book in Old Town, Corktown and Distillery districts. The latter is a buzzing spot for restaurants, galleries, specialty boutiques and live music.

Useful Websites

Tourism Toronto (www.seetorontonow.com) Official city tourism website with loads of info, including top lists.

blogTO (www.blogto.com) The go-to blog, with up-to-date info on local happenings – city-wide and by neighborhood.

Toronto Life (https://torontolife.com) Excellent lifestyle magazine with restaurant reviews and event listings.

NEED TO KNOW

CURRENCY
Canadian dollar ($)

LANGUAGES
English, French

VISAS
Visitors may require a visa to enter Canada. Those exempt require an Electronic Travel Authorization (eTA; $7), with the exception of Americans. See www.cic.gc.ca/english/visit/eta-start.asp.

FUEL
Gas is sold in liters on major highways. Expect to pay around $1.80 to $2 per liter, with higher prices in more remote areas.

RENTAL CARS
Be sure to have an international license if you're not from an English- or French-speaking country.

Budget (www.budget.com)

Hertz (www.hertz.com)

Practicar (www.practicar.ca)

Thrifty (www.thrifty canada.ca)

IMPORTANT NUMBERS
Emergency (☎911)
Ambulance, police, fire, mountain rescue, coast guard.

Roadside assistance (☎1 800-222-4357)

Climate

Dry climate
Warm to hot summers, mild winters
Summers – mild to warm (north & east) & warm to hot (south), cold winters
Polar climate

Churchill
GO Sep–Nov

Banff
GO Jul–Sep

Vancouver
GO Jun–Aug

Halifax
GO Jul–Sep

Montréal
GO Jun–Aug

Toronto
GO Jun–Aug

When to Go

High Season (Jun–Aug)
» Sunshine and warm weather prevail; far northern regions briefly thaw.

» Accommodation prices peak (up 30% on average).

» December through March is equally busy and expensive in ski-resort towns.

Shoulder (May, Sep & Oct)
» Crowds and prices drop off.

» Temperatures are cool but comfortable.

» Attractions keep shorter hours.

» Fall-foliage areas (eg Cape Breton Island and Québec) remain busy.

Low Season (Nov–Apr)
» Places outside the big cities and ski resorts close.

» Darkness and cold take over.

» April and November are particularly good for bargains.

Your Daily Budget

Budget: Less than $100
» Dorm bed: $25–40
» Campsite: $25–35
» Self-catered meals from markets and supermarkets: $12–20

Midrange: $100–250
» B&B room: $80–180 ($100–250 in major cities)
» Meal in a good local restaurant: from $20 plus drinks
» Rental car: per day $45–70

Top end: More than $250
» Four-star hotel room: from $180
» Three-course meal in a top restaurant: from $65 plus drinks
» Skiing day pass: $50–90

Eating

Cafes Often serve sandwiches, soups and baked goods, as well as coffee.

Diners Brunches and lunches, sometimes served 24 hours; often family-friendly.

Pubs Home-cooked fish and chips, burgers and salads.

Vegetarians Options are decent outside of rural areas.

The following price ranges are for main dishes.

$	less than $15
$$	$15–$25
$$$	more than $25

Sleeping

B&Bs Purpose-built villas to heritage homes, they are often atmospheric.

Motels Good-value options dotting the highways into town.

Hostels Traveler hangouts, favored by outdoor adventurers in remoter regions.

Camping Campgrounds are plentiful.

The following price ranges refer to a double room with private bathroom in high season, excluding tax (which can be up to 17%).

$	less than $100
$$	$100–$250
$$$	more than $250

Arriving in Canada

Toronto Pearson International Airport Trains (adult/child $12.35/free) run downtown every 15 minutes from 5:30am to 1am; taxis cost around $60 (45 minutes).

Montréal Trudeau International Airport A 24-hour airport shuttle bus ($10) runs downtown. Taxis cost a flat $40 (30 to 60 minutes).

Vancouver International Airport Trains ($7.95 to $10.70) run downtown every six to 20 minutes; taxis cost around $40 (30 minutes).

Land Border Crossings The Canadian Border Services Agency (www.cbsa-asfc.gc.ca/bwt-taf/menu-eng.html) posts wait times (usually 30 minutes).

Cell Phones

Local SIM cards can be used in unlocked GSM 850/1900 compatible phones. Other phones must be set to roaming. Coverage is spotty.

Internet Access

Wi-fi is widely available in hotels, cafes and many restaurants.

Money

ATMs are widely available. Credit cards are accepted in nearly all hotels and restaurants.

Tipping

Tipping is a standard practice. Generally you can expect to tip:

Restaurant waitstaff 15% to 20%

Bar staff $1 per drink

Hotel bellhop $1 to $2 per bag

Hotel-room cleaners From $2 per day

Taxis 10% to 15%

Useful Websites

Destination Canada (en.destinationcanada.com) Official tourism site.

Environment Canada Weather (www.weather.gc.ca) Forecasts for any town.

Lonely Planet (www.lonelyplanet.com/canada) Destination information, hotel recommendations and more.

Government of Canada (www.gc.ca) National and regional information.

Parks Canada (www.pc.gc.ca) Lowdown on national parks.

Canadian Broadcasting Corporation (www.cbc.ca) National and provincial news.

For more, see Road Trip Essentials (p110).

13

Road Trips

1 **The Niagara Peninsula** 3 Days
Explore vineyards, botanical gardens and one awe-inspiring set of waterfalls. (p17)

2 **Lake Superior Coastline** 7 Days
Take in islands, forested reserves and sandy beaches on this photogenic lakeside drive. (p27)

3 **Eastern Townships** 1 Day
Discover forested lakes, rolling vineyards, fine food and antique markets. (p35)

4 **Around, Over & In the St Lawrence River** 3 Days
Eat local delicacies on the Île d'Orléans, feel the power of thundering Montmorency Falls and spot wildlife on Cap Tourmente. (p45)

Montmorency Falls, Parc de la Chute-Montmorency (p48)
MD GOMES/SHUTTERSTOCK ©

The Niagara Peninsula

A trip through the Niagara Peninsula will offer majestic views, historic sights, vineyards and even a casino — perfect for a short getaway or a side trip from Toronto.

TRIP HIGHLIGHTS

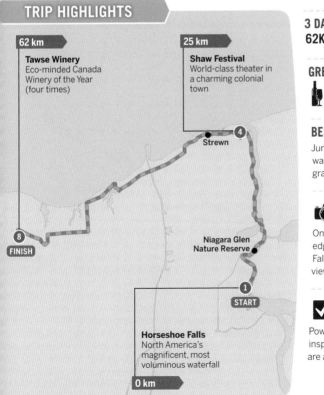

62 km

Tawse Winery
Eco-minded Canada Winery of the Year (four times)

25 km

Shaw Festival
World-class theater in a charming colonial town

Strewn

4

8
FINISH

Niagara Glen
Nature Reserve

1
START

Horseshoe Falls
North America's magnificent, most voluminous waterfall

0 km

**3 DAYS
62KM/39 MILES**

GREAT FOR...

BEST TIME TO GO
June to September for warm days and the grape-harvest season.

ESSENTIAL PHOTO
On the thundering edge of Horseshoe Falls, from Table Rock viewpoint.

BEST FOR WATERFALLS
Powerful and awe-inspiring, Niagara Falls are a must-see.

1 The Niagara Peninsula

The Niagara Peninsula is a feast for the senses. The thunder of water as it cascades over a towering cliff; the delicate brush of mist during a catamaran trip along the falls; the sight of a colonial-era soldier prepping a musket for battle; the cheers and applause at Ontario's most celebrated stages; and the sweet, viscous flavors of ice wine, grown in vineyards stretching as far as the eye can see.

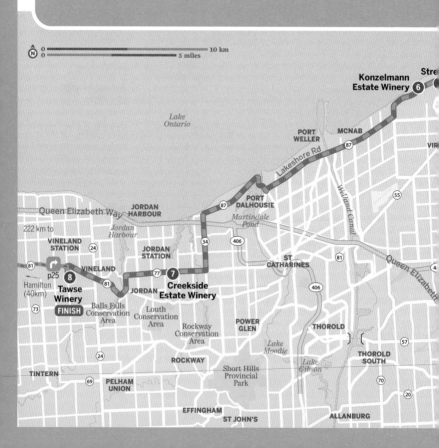

❶ Niagara Falls (p70)

Horseshoe Falls is the shining star of the town of Niagara Falls – a 670m-wide, U-shaped waterfall, North America's highest-volume cascade, moving 8500 bathtubs worth of water per second over its ridges to the frothing Maid of the Mist Pool below. Enjoy the magnificent views and the falls' cooling mist from **Table Rock** viewpoint. Afterward, walk north for 1km along the curving Niagara Park-way, taking in the views of the smaller but still impressive **American Falls** and **Bridal Veil Falls**, to the **Hornblower Niagara Cruise** (www.niagaracruises.com; 5920 Niagara Pkwy; adult/child $26/16, fireworks cruise $40; ⊙8:30am-8:30pm May-Sep, to 5:30pm Oct) port. Here, a 20-minute cata-maran ride gets you up-close-and-personal with all three of Niagara Falls' cascades; prepare to don a poncho and somehow still get drenched. After this, dry off as you walk up the hill to the 158m **Skylon Tower** (☎905-356-2651; www.skylon.com; 5200 Robinson St; adult/child $16.25/10.50; ⊙9am-10pm Mon-Thu, to 11pm Fri-Sun; **P**), with its jaw-dropping views of the falls and, on a clear day, Toronto. For some grown-up fun, try your luck at **Niagara Falls-view Casino** (☎888-325-5788; www.fallsviewcasinoresort.com; 6380 Fallsview Blvd; ⊙24hr) across the street. Jackpots won, head to the **Niagara Falls History Museum** (☎905-358-5082; https://niagarafallsmuseums.

ca; 5810 Ferry St; adult/child $5/4, Thu 5-9pm free; ⊙10am-5pm Tue, Wed & Fri-Sun, to 9pm Thu; **P** 🚻), 1.5km northwest on Ferry St. A well-curated museum, it has excellent multimedia exhibits on the transfor-mation of the area from an Indigenous settlement to a modern-day tourist zone; stories of daredevils and coverage of the War of 1812 are especially en-gaging. End your visit in famously kitschy **Clifton Hill**, 1.5 km east, a street filled with wax museums, creepy fun houses and arcades. Unsurprisingly for such a big tourist draw, there's plenty of eating and accommoda-tion options.

The Drive » Follow Niagara Parkway north for 8km, winding along the verdant road that Winston Churchill once described as 'the prettiest Sunday afternoon drive in the world.' On one side, you'll see souvenir shops eventually give way to Victorian-era homes; on the other, the grassy cliffs above the Niagara River and the Niagara River Recreation Trail that runs alongside it.

TOP TIP: HORSESHOE FALLS PHOTO OP

A little-known but great spot to take a photo of Horseshoe Falls is inside the **Table Rock Visitor Centre**. Head to the 2nd floor and you'll find a bank of floor-to-ceiling windows high enough to overlook the falls and the crowds in front of it. It's a magazine-worthy vista!

❷ Niagara Glen Nature Reserve

This **Nature Reserve**
(☎905-354-6678; www.niagara
parks.com; 3050 Niagara Pkwy;
⊙Reserve dawn-dusk, Nature
Centre 10am-5pm Apr-Nov;
🅿 ♿) is a local hikers' fave
with 4km of trails leading
through the Carolinian
forest, down the gorge to
the fast-moving Niagara
River. Start at the **Nature
Center**, to get a trail map
and to learn about the
terrain, flora and fauna.
Then take the 17m-high
steel staircase to the start
of the trail system. At the
bottom, turn north (left)
on the **Cliffside Trail** to
Terrace Trail, a short but
steep hike with massive
boulders and stone steps
that lead to **River Trail**.
Head south (right) along
the relatively flat trail to
take in the beech trees,
the white-capped river
and the towering gorge
walls. Finally, dog-leg
on **Eddy Trail** to take the
challenging **Whirlpool
Trail** (expect boulders and
uneven terrain) to the
fast and furious whirlpool
in the river (look for the
gondola) or just loop back
to the Cliffside Trail, to
head back.

The Drive ≫ Continue 650m
north along Niagara Pkwy.

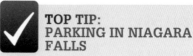

**TOP TIP:
PARKING IN NIAGARA
FALLS**

Parking is limited and expensive in Niagara Falls.
Before handing over a bucket of cash at a random lot,
swing by the **Niagara IMAX Theatre** (☎905-358-3611;
www.imaxniagara.com; 6170 Fallsview Blvd; IMAX adult/child
$13/9.50, Daredevil Exhibit adult/child $8/6.50, combo adult/
child $15.50/13; ⊙9am-9pm; 🅿 ♿). It has an open-air lot
next to the Skylon, and its parking rates are typically a
steal – around $10 per day – and the location is tops.

NIAGARA FALLS & HYDROELECTRIC POWER

Though nowhere near the tallest waterfalls in the world (that honor goes to 979m
Angel Falls in Venezuela), Niagara Falls is one of the world's most voluminous, with
more than 168,000 cubic meters of water going over its crest lines every minute. At
least, that is, from 8am to 10pm during the peak tourist season, April to September.

In fact, the water making it over the falls – Horseshoe, American and Bridal
Veil – only accounts for 25 to 50% of their capacity. The rest is diverted into
hydroelectric plants on both sides of the border, depending on the time of day and
year: Sir Andrew Beck Station Stations #1 and #2 in Ontario and Robert Moses
Hydro Electric Plant in New York. Built across from each other, the hydroelectric
plants divert water from the Niagara River using a system of gates located 2.6km
before the falls. The water is run through hydro tunnels on both sides of the border
to turbines that generate electricity; the water is eventually returned to the Niagara
River, just above Lake Ontario. The entire process is governed under the 1950
Niagara Treaty, an international agreement that assures water levels and a fair
division of electricity (Ontario actually gets a little more). Power generated from
the Niagara River accounts for 25% of all electricity used in Ontario and New York
State – a remarkable figure, especially considering Toronto and New York City are
included. For visitors to Niagara Falls this means that, depending on the time of day
and year, the falls may appear more or less voluminous. The highest volume any
time of year is from April 1 to October 31, during daylight hours. The rest of the year,
or at night, the falls look remarkably smaller but the street lights, somehow, seem to
shine a little brighter.

Butterfly Conservatory

③ Botanical Gardens & Butterfly Conservatory

Forty hectares of beautifully landscaped gardens filled with thousands of perennials, sculpted shrubs and towering trees make the **Botanical Gardens** (☏905-356-8119; www.niagaraparks.com; 2565 Niagara Pkwy; butterfly conservatory adult/child $16/10.25, gardens free; ⏰10am-4pm Mon-Fri, to 5pm Sat & Sun Sep-Jun, 10am-7pm Sun-Wed, to 8pm Thu-Sat Jul & Aug; 🅿 👫) a visually inspiring and soothing stop. Meander along the leafy paths, passing the parterre garden and the must-see Victorian rose garden with more than 2400 roses – a popular photo op. In the central part of the gardens sits the **Butterfly Conservatory**, a high-glass-domed building with a rainforest-like setting – plants, waterfalls, heat and all – with more than 2000 delicate butterflies flitting about, often landing on visitors. Of the 45 species of butterflies living here, 60% are from Costa Rica, El Salvador and the Philippines; the rest are raised in an on-site greenhouse.

The Drive ≫ Continue 15km north on the leisurely Niagara Parkway, passing the Floral Clock, a popular pit stop for photos. As you travel north, the houses become grander, the parkway less crowded and vineyards begin to dot the landscape. Eventually, Niagara Parkway becomes Queen's Parade.

④ Niagara-on-the-Lake (p74)

As you enter the pretty colonial town of Niagara-on-the-Lake, the spiked walls of **Fort George** (www.pc.gc.ca/fortgeorge; 51 Queens Pde; adult/child $11.70/free; ⏰10am-5pm May-Oct, noon-4pm Sat & Sun only Nov-Apr; 🅿 👫) appear on your right. Dating to 1797, it was the site of several bloody battles during the War of 1812. Wander among well-restored buildings, watch musket demonstrations and learn about daily life

WHY THIS IS A CLASSIC TRIP
LIZA PRADO, WRITER

This trip takes you to one of Canada's most iconic sites: Niagara Falls, a thundering, awe-inspiring set of cascades. Few people realize you can experience them on land, water, and even from high above. But the Niagara Peninsula offers more than the falls – including an exploration of leafy trails and botanical gardens, a beautiful colonial town and a landscape of vineyards.

Above: Niagara-on-the-Lake (p21)
Left: Konzelmann Estate Winery (24)
Right: Botanical Gardens & Butterfly Conservatory (p21)

here from chipper staff in historic dress. Just north on Queen's Parade sits the main theater of the **Shaw Festival** (www. shawfest.com; 10 Queens Pde; ⊙Apr-Dec, box office 9am-9pm). A highly respected and popular theater company, it's named after the playwright George Bernard Shaw, whose plays were showcased during the company's first season in 1962. Today, the festival stages plays and musicals from the Victorian era to the modern day in three theaters around town. From here, head two blocks north on Queen's St (aka Queen's Parade) to the **clock tower**, a WWI memorial. This marks the center of town, an area with flower-lined streets, 19th-century-storefront boutiques and colonial-era homes. Window shop and explore!

The Drive » Head northwest on Mary St, a road that runs parallel to Queen St, five blocks away. Stay on the small road – which becomes Lakeshore Dr – for 5km, as it winds through verdant countryside, passing modest homes and vineyards.

----

❺ Niagara-on-the-Lake Wine Country: Strewn

Tucked into the west side of Lakeshore Dr is **Strewn** (☏905-468-1229; www.strewnwinery.com; 1339 Lakeshore Rd; tastings $10-15; ⊙10am-6pm). The building itself isn't particularly charming – a modernized and expanded canning facility – but the wines are award-winning and the staff welcoming. Pop in for a wine tasting – its oaky Terroir Chardonnay and sweet Gewurztraminer are the ones you can't miss.

In the summer, consider booking a class at its modern **Wine Country Cooking School** (☎905-468-8304; www.winecountrycooking.com; 1339 Lakeshore Rd; classes from $225; ◷10am-3pm or 4-9pm Sat) to hone your cooking skills or to learn new dishes that pair well with wines.

The Drive ❯❯ Continue northwest on Lakeshore Dr for 1km.

❻ Niagara-on-the-Lake Wine Country: Konzelmann Estate Winery

On the east side of Lakeshore Dr sits **Konzelmann Estate Winery** (☎905-935-2866; www.konzelmann.ca; 1096 Lakeshore Rd; tours $10-35; ◷10am-6pm, tours May-Sep), one of the oldest vineyards in the region (established 1984) and the only one set on Lake Ontario. The views over its vineyards to Toronto's skyline are spectacular. Tours of its facilities, including tastings in its elegant, chateau-like building, are a treat. The late-harvest Vidal and ice wines are the ticket here.

The Drive ❯❯ Continue on Lakeshore Dr for 17km, passing over the Welland Canal and through the town of Port Dalhousie until it meets Rte 34. Turn left and continue for 3.4km, passing over Queen Elizabeth Way (QEW) highway, vineyards and orchards of Twenty Valley Wine Country dotting the landscape. At Rte 77, a quiet country road, turn right and drive for 2km.

❼ Twenty Valley Wine Country: Creekside Estate Winery

A modest entrance belies the spunky and entrepreneurial spirit of **Creekside Estate Winery** (☎905-562-0035; www.creeksidewine.com; 2170 4th Ave, Jordan Station; tastings from $10, tours $12;

💬 LOCAL KNOWLEDGE: WINE FESTIVALS

Niagara Peninsula is home to several wine-related festivals (www.niagarawinefestival.com and www.twentyvalley.ca) throughout the year. Time your visit to be able to attend one of these locals' faves in the wine country of Niagara-on-the-Lake and its neighbor Twenty Valley:

Niagara Homegrown Wine Festival (June) Kicks off Niagara's summer wine-tasting season with two weekends of wine-and-food-pairing events; typically more than 30 wineries participate.

Niagara Grape and Wine Festival (September) Celebrates the harvest season with two weeks of wine tastings and concerts around the region as well as two parades in St Catherines.

Niagara Icewine Festival (January) Showcases Ontario's stickiest, sweetest ice wines during a 16-day winter festival, including winery tours, street festivals and a gala party at the Niagara Fallsview Casino (p19).

Twenty Valley Winter WineFest (January) Celebrates Twenty Valley wines in Jordan Village during one weekend of tastings, live music and outdoor events like ice-wine-puck shoot-outs and barrel-rolling competitions.

DETOUR:
HAMILTON ART SCENE

Start: ⑧ Twenty Valley Wine Country: Tawse Winery

Once a gritty steel-industry hub, downtown Hamilton today has a welcoming air and a burgeoning arts scene. James St N is a good place to explore, with its independent galleries, quirky boutiques and hipster eateries. On the second Friday of each month, James St hosts **Hamilton Art Crawl** (https://tourismhamilton.com; James St N; ⊙7-10pm), a veritable party zone when crowds of locals and visitors meander among galleries and shops that are open late, art studios with open doors and street performers doing their thing.

If quiet art appreciation is more your style, pop into the **Art Gallery of Hamilton** (AGH; ☎905-527-6610; www.artgalleryofhamilton.com; 123 King St W; special exhibitions adult/child $13.25/8.85, free 1st Fri of month; ⊙11am-6pm Wed & Fri, to 8pm Thu, noon-5pm Sat-Sun, to 8pm first Fri of month; P) instead. A sleek affair in the heart of downtown, the collection focuses on modern and 19th-century Canadian art. The gallery offers free tours, led by knowledgeable docents, covering the highlights and hidden gems of the collection; offered at 1pm on Wednesdays and on weekends, the tours are highly recommended if you can swing it. Afterward, stop for lunch at the nearby **Hamilton's Farmers Market** (☎905-546-2096; https://hamiltonfarmersmarket.ca; 35 York Blvd; ⊙8am-6pm Tue, Thu & Fri, 7am-5pm Sat; P ☎). You'll find vendors selling fresh and local produce, meat and bread of all sorts at this 180-year-old market; head to the ground level for a remarkable variety of international fast-food eateries, a snapshot of the diversity of this town.

A stop in Hamilton is best done at the beginning or end of your Niagara Peninsula tour. Located just off the QEW, it's a quick jaunt to **Tawse**, just 43km away.

⊙10am-6pm May-Nov, 11am-5pm Dec-Apr, tours at 2pm May-Oct). Come here for a down-and-dirty tour of the cellars and vineyards (really, bring boots) or an afternoon on the patio with live music and a glass of wine in hand. It can also provide picnic lunches to enjoy in the vineyards, including a blanket and wine. Try the Sauvignon Blanc and Syrah, the focus of Creekside's experimental wine portfolio.

The Drive » Turn left on Rte 77, continuing until 19th St. Turn left, passing through the charming village of Jordan; immediately after Jordan House, turn right on King St. Stay on King St for about 4.5km as it curves through farmland and over creeks, eventually passing the outskirts of Vineland. Turn left on Cherry Av, staying on it for just 0.6km.

- - - - - - - - - - - - - - - - - -

⑧ Twenty Valley Wine Country: Tawse Winery

A four-time Canada Winery of the Year winner, **Tawse** (☎905-562-9500; www.tawsewinery.ca; 3955 Cherry Ave, Vineland; tastings $8, tours $15; ⊙10am-6pm May-Oct, to 5pm Nov-Apr) is a must-stop. Sitting on a rise, its elegant tasting room opens to fields of grapes. Known for its organic wines – the chardonnay is over-the-top delicious – Tawse uses a biodynamic approach to farming, utilizing the land's natural cycles and animals like sheep and chickens that feed on leaves and bugs to keep its soil and vines healthy. A tour of the facilities, including tastings, is interesting and worthwhile.

Lake Superior Coastline

On this drive packed with forest and coastlines, you'll experience friendly locals, stunning scenery and abundant wildlife.

2

TRIP HIGHLIGHTS

1691 km

Kenora
Forests, lakes, canoes, and good beer

977 km

Slate Islands
Herds of caribou congregating on an island formed by an ancient meteorite

7
FINISH

5

Thunder Bay

Lake Superior Provincial Park

START
Sudbury

2

Killarney Provincial Park
Paddling, hiking and wildlife in a peaceful park

100 km

---

7 DAYS
1691KM/
1051 MILES

GREAT FOR...

BEST TIME TO GO

June to September for sunny weather and lack of snow on the roads.

ESSENTIAL PHOTO

In front of the lighthouse on Slate Island.

BEST FOR OUTDOORS

Canoeing in Killarney Provincial Park.

---

2 Lake Superior Coastline

There will be times on this route when you won't see another car for hours. And that's part of the appeal – enjoy the solitude while cruising alongside Lake Superior, keeping an eye out for moose.

① Sudbury (p76)

While Sudbury is not the most idyllic town in northwestern Ontario, it is an important stop to understand what makes this part of the province tick: mining. Most towns in the region started as mining towns and Sudbury's **Dynamic Earth** (📞705-522-3701; www.dynamicearth.ca; 122 Big Nickel Rd; adult/child $22/18, parking $6 in summer; ⊙9am-6pm Apr-Oct) museum is a great intro to nickel mining and the area's history. Be sure to get your picture

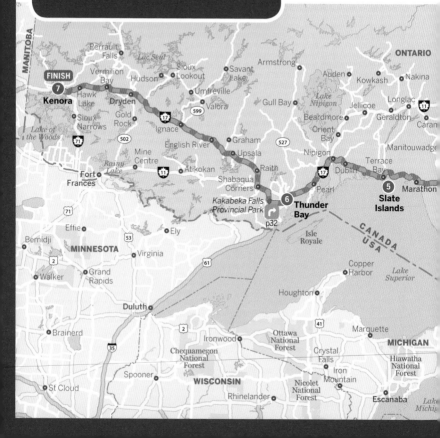

in front of the Big Nickel, a 9m-high stainless steel replica of a 1951 Canadian nickel ($0.05).

If geology is not your thing, Sudbury has a burgeoning food scene. It's easy to while away the rest of the day at **46 North Brewing Corp** (📞705-586-1870; www.46north.ca; 1275 Kelly Lake Rd; ⏰11am-7pm Tue-Sat) followed by dinner at the **Respect is Burning** (📞705-675-5777; www.ribsupperclub.com; 82 Durham St; mains $19-35; ⏰5-10pm Mon-Thu, to 1am Fri & Sat; 📶) supper club.

The Drive » Be on the lookout for moose and other wildlife on the 100km drive to Killarney Provincial Park, particularly after turning onto Hwy 637 from the Trans-Canada Hwy. The road is quite simple to follow; just keep driving until you reach the park gate.

----

② Killarney Provincial Park (p75)

Killarney Provincial Park (📞705-287-2900; www.ontarioparks.com/park/killarney; Hwy 637; day use per vehicle $13, campsite $37-53, backcountry camping adult/child under 18yr $12.50/6, yurt $98, cabin $142; ⏰year-round)

is an outdoor lovers' dream, with 645 sq km of nature. There is a variety of hikes, from the 80km La Cloche Silhouette Trail for experienced hikers to a short 2km loop on the Granite Ridge Trail. This trail also offers great views of the La Cloche mountains and climbs to a lookout point on a ridge overlooking the park.

Those looking to really get away from it all can rent a canoe from **Killarney Kanoes** (📞888-461-4446, toll-free 705-287-2197; www.killarneykanoes.com; 1611 Bell Lake Rd; canoe rental per day $27-43; ⏰8am-8pm May-Oct) and explore the many lakes in the park. Most people canoe around Bell Lake, but you can also rent canoes at George Lake, Carlyle Lake and Johnny Lake access points. Spend the night at Killarney Mountain Lodge (p76), unwinding in the sauna after your day in nature.

The Drive » It's next to impossible to get lost driving in northwestern Ontario as there's only one main route. To get to Sault Ste Marie, follow Hwy 637 for 65km until you reach the Trans-Canada Hwy, turn right and follow Hwy 17 for around 350km to reach 'the Soo'.

----

③ Sault Ste Marie

A stopover in Sault Ste Marie is like a rite of passage for northern Ontario road trippers. It's not the prettiest city, but it is a friendly place with loads of character. Stay

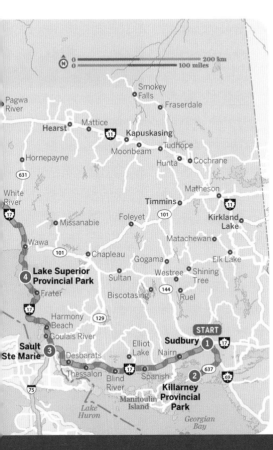

over at the Water Tower Inn (p78) where the kids can play in the pools and there's a pub for the parents. There isn't much nightlife here, but that's a good thing because you'll need to get up early the following day if you're keen to make a day trip through the Lake Superior forest on the **Agawa Canyon Tour Train** (ACR; ✆855-768-4171, reservations 800-461-6020; www.agawatrain.com; 129 Bay St; adult/child $101/55; ⊙late Jun–mid-Oct). It departs at 8am and returns at 6pm and is a must-do in autumn as the foliage turns to magnificent shades of red and orange.

The Drive » The 120km drive to Lake Superior Provincial Park is where you really start to get a feel for the region. Follow Hwy 17 as it hugs the coast, offering fleeting glimpses of the sparkling lake through the forest. Stop in at Harmony Beach if the sun is shining to stretch your legs.

❹ Lake Superior Provincial Park (p78)

The fjord-like passages, thick evergreen forest and sandy beaches of

Lake Superior Provincial Park (✆park office 705-856-2284, visitors centre 705-882-2026; www.ontarioparks.com/park/lakesuperior; Hwy 17; day use per vehicle $14.50/5.25/7.50, campsites $42-47, backcountry camping adult/child $10.17/5.09; ⊙Agawa Bay Visitors Centre 9am-8pm Jun-Sep, to 5pm late May & early Oct) are straight out of a postcard. The highway runs right through the park, but it's well worth stopping to check out the hiking routes. The **Twilight Resort** (✆705-882-2183; www.facebook.com/twilighttesort; Hwy 17, Montreal River Harbour; tent sites $30-42, cabins from $100; ⊙May-Oct) is situated just before the park and is a great base for exploration.

If you can drag yourself away from the resort and its idyllic views of Lake Superior, enter the park and head to the Agawa Bay Visitors Centre, which is 9km from the southern boundary. The friendly staff can advise you on hiking and take you out to the Agawa Rock Pictographs. The ochre-red drawings are

a spiritual site for the Ojibwe and are reported to be between 150 and 400 years old.

The Drive » One of the most picturesque drives in Ontario, the 360km drive to Terrace Bay cuts through Lake Superior Provincial Park. The road forks after the park – keep left to stay on Hwy 17 instead of heading into Wawa on Hwy 101. You'll head into the countryside before veering west again to Terrace Bay, the base for visiting the Slate Islands.

❺ Slate Islands (p79)

Formed by an ancient meteorite, inhabited by herds of woodland

TOP TIP:
GAS STATIONS

Hwy 17 is fairly well serviced, but it's still a long route. Be sure to fill up whenever you fall below the half-way point to make sure you don't get stuck. Gas is also much cheaper on Indigenous reserves, of which there are many in northern Ontario.

Sudbury (p28) The Big Nickel

caribou and featuring pristine paddling opportunities... Need we say more? The **Slate Islands** (📞807-825-3403; www.ontarioparks.com/park/slateislands), located 13km south of Terrace Bay, is one of the top places in the region for a unique experience. Either grab a ferry, or sign up for a paddling tour with **Naturally Superior Adventures** (📞800-203-9092, 705-856-2939; www.naturallysuperior.com; 10 Government Dock Rd, Lake Superior; courses from $50, day trips from $137). Don't forget your camera as caribou sightings are virtually guaranteed,

and you'll no doubt want a selfie in front of the 100-year-old lighthouse. Geology buffs will also love the 'shatter cones', conical shapes in the rocks formed by the impact of a meteorite 400-800 million years ago.

The Drive » You can get to the Slate Islands from Terrace Bay either by ferry or your own paddling steam. Once back from the islands, the trip to the next stop is fairly straightforward – follow Hwy 17 for 220km until you reach Thunder Bay.

----

6 Thunder Bay (p80)

For a long time, Thunder Bay was referred to by

road trippers as 'a wonderful place to drive through.' Until recently, there were few reasons to stop in the city other than to sleep. But a food culture has emerged in this isolated city. **Tomlin** (www.tomlinrestaurant.com; 202 Red River Rd; mains $16-28, cocktails $10-14; ⊙5-10pm Tue-Sat) serves some of the best food this side of Toronto, and the **Sleeping Giant Brewing Co.** (www.sleepinggiantbrewing.ca; 712 Macdonell St; ⊙11am-10pm Mon-Sat, from noon Sun; 📶) makes great ales and lagers, which you'll find all around town. On top of being an ideal base for exploring the vast forests

DETOUR:
KAKABEKA FALLS PROVINCIAL PARK

Start: ⑥ **Thunder Bay**

Kakabeka Falls Provincial Park (☎807-473-9231; www.ontarioparks.com/park/
kakabekafalls; Hwy 11-17; day use per vehicle $11.25) is a very short, but worthwhile detour
on your trip from Thunder Bay to Kenora. The 40m-high waterfall is one of Ontario's
highest and is quite stunning to view in early spring during the thaw, but also
amazing to observe in winter when the falls are encrusted in thick ice. There are also
hiking trails in the park, including parts of the 1.3km hike that were historically used
by the first Europeans in Canada to portage around the falls.

The falls are also important in Ojibwe folklore. Legend has it that Green Mantle, an
Ojibwe princess, pretended to be lost in the region to fool the rival Sioux, who were
preparing for an attack, and then led them to their deaths over the falls to prevent the
massacre. It's said that you can see Princess Green Mantle when looking into the mist
of the falls. From Thunder Bay, drive along Hwy 11/17 on the way to Kenora for 29km
until you see a turnoff to the left towards the falls. To rejoin the main trip, just exit the
park and turn left – you'll be back on the main highway and heading towards Kenora.

and lakes in northern
Ontario, Thunder Bay also
offers local hiking up **Mt
McKay** (www.fwfn.com; Mission Rd; per vehicle $5; ⊘9am-
10pm mid-May–early Oct). You
can also learn more about
the region's history at **Fort
William Historical Park**
(www.fwhp.ca; 1350 King Rd;
adult/child $14/10; ⊘10am-
5pm mid-May–mid-Sep, tours
every 45min).

The Drive » Take Hwy 17 out
of Thunder Bay, which is called
Hwy 11/17, for close to 500km
until you reach Kenora. There
will be one major split in the
road, where Hwy 11 veers off
towards Atikokan – stay right.

⑦ Kenora

Our final stop brings you
to the end of northern
Ontario before you
either head back or on
to Winnipeg, Manitoba.
It's a quaint little town
known for its cottages,
lakes and hunting. On
the drive, be sure to stop
at **Busters Barbeque**
(www.bustersbbq.com; Fort
Vermillion, Hwy 17; mains
$10-16; ⊘11am-8pm May-Sep;
🅿 👬 😺) in Vermilion Bay
for a good ol' Canadian
BBQ lunch (about 100km
before Kenora) and then
adjourn for the day by

the lake or at **Lake of the
Woods Brewing Com-
pany** (☎807-468-2337; www.
lowbrewco.com; 350 Second
St, Kenora; ⊘11am-12am
Mon-Wed, to 1am Thu-Fri May-
Sep, 11am-11pm Oct-Apr; 🛜)
for some beers and more
BBQ. If you don't feel like
paddling yourself around
the many small lakes
and inlets, take a sunset
dinner cruise on the **MS
Kenora** (www.mskenora.
com; Off Bernier Dr; adult/child
3-10yr $31/17; ⊘May-Sep) to
explore a fraction of the
14,500 islands that dot
the Lake of the Woods.

Kakabeka Falls
MARC GUITARD/GETTY IMAGES©

Eastern Townships

On this lake-villages drive you'll witness classic Québécois life in the region's Eastern Townships, with colorful wooden homes, sparkling lakes and ponds, maple-syrup-heavy cafes and interesting wineries.

3

TRIP HIGHLIGHTS

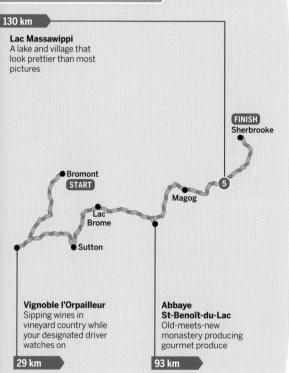

130 km

Lac Massawippi
A lake and village that look prettier than most pictures

FINISH
Sherbrooke

● Bromont
START

Lac Brome

● Sutton

Magog

5

Vignoble l'Orpailleur
Sipping wines in vineyard country while your designated driver watches on

29 km

Abbaye St-Benoît-du-Lac
Old-meets-new monastery producing gourmet produce

93 km

1 DAY
153KM/95 MILES

GREAT FOR...

BEST TIME TO GO
June and July has sunny weather with less traffic than in August.

ESSENTIAL PHOTO
At Abbaye St-Benoît-du-Lac with Lac Memphrémagog in the background.

BEST FOR CULTURE
Antique-store hopping for a glimpse of another era.

Eastern Townships

This is a trip for people who like to take things at a leisurely pace, to experience local Québécois life with all its quirks – local produce, including cider and cheese made by monks, lakeside towns with duck festivals, and a treasure hunt of open-air murals. Between all the eccentricities, the ride is smooth and carefree.

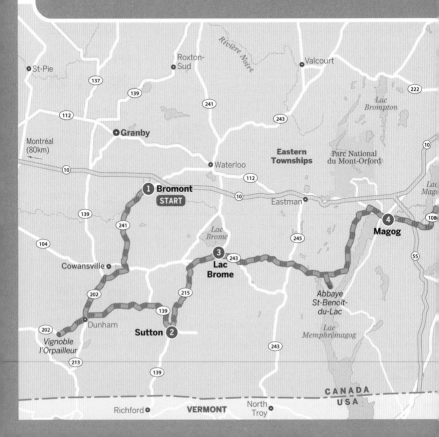

1 Bromont (p95)

From Montréal's Champlain Bridge take Hwy 10 for 75km and take Exit 78 to central Bromont. The ever-changing palette of Mt Brome is the highlight of stopping in this town. In winter its pines are laden with snow, luring skiers to **Ski Bromont** (☎450-534-2200; www.ski bromont.com; 150 Rue Champlain; full/half day $42/34; 🎿) with its roughly 140 trails, including almost 100 trails open for night skiing. In warmer weather the resort hosts

a water park with fun slides, and its 100km of marked trails, including 15 thrilling downhill routes, have made it a mecca for mountain-bike aficionados (Bromont has hosted world championships). Even if you don't stop for long, a cruise by the edges of the 553m-high mount is a fine start to the journey into the region and its history – Mt Brome is what remains of an ancient series of volcanoes. If that sounds too active, you might prefer to indulge with treats such as chocolate-covered cherries at the **Musée du Chocolat de la Confiserie Bromont** (☎450-534-3893; www.lemuseeduchocolatdela confiseriebromont.com; 679 Rue Shefford; meals from $13.25; ⏰8am-5pm). Its museum covers the history and process of chocolate making. And vegans can enjoy the taste sensations at Gaïa Resto Végan (p95).

The Drive » Head south for 35km through Cowansville to Vignoble l'Orpailleur, a flat drive through the region's wineries and flat-flat houses with pruned lawns. As you head east from the wineries to Sutton, the 60km of road rise and there are three crossroads without any large signage. Instead, look for the small street signs to decide which street to follow.

2 Sutton (p95)

This is wine country and the most prestigious vineyard of them all, **Vignoble l'Orpailleur** (☎450-295-

2763; http://orpailleur.ca; 1086 Rue Bruce, Dunham; ⏰10am-4:30pm), has a quirky display on the history of alcohol in Québec and offers wine tasting year-round. The vineyard was established in 1982, but l'Orpailleur has pedigree – two of those in charge of the vines are sons of winemakers. The flat greenery is worth a peek, even if you are the designated driver. It has an attached restaurant, too.

Pause for a stroll through relaxed and beautiful Sutton and to linger at one of its cheery cafes, or reserve a romantic room at Le Pleasant Hôtel & Café (p96). You might spot skiers getting warm after a trip to Mont Sutton during the winter, and hikers recovering from the climbs and rough camping on **Parc d'Environnement Naturel** (☎450-538-4085; www.parcsutton.com; adult/child $6/3; ⏰Jun-Oct; 🎿).

The Drive » The easy 18km drive northeast to Lac Brome is along Rte 215. In the south, the trees are sparser with grasslands and lawns stretching out into the distance. As you approach the town, you'll know it because of the mansion-like homes beaming as if recently painted, and pine trees on large lawns as if every day were Christmas.

3 Lac Brome (p95)

The traditional village-life essence of the Eastern Townships is surely encapsulated in downtown Lac Brome, the name given to a town made up of seven villages that converge on a lake of the same name. The town is home to the well-heeled, so the stores here cater to fine tastes with boutique clothing and gift stores, and more than a dozen well-curated antiques. Many stores are in converted Victorian houses, so there is a British flavor

of yesteryear that is part of the highlight of stopping here. Stroll the lake and pop in for the area's famous duck products at **Brome Lake Duck Farm** (☎450-242-3825; www.canardsdulacbrome.com; 40 Chemin Centre; ◷8am-5pm Mon-Thu, to 6pm Fri, 9am-6pm Sat, 10am-5pm Sun). Lac Brome's prettiest village, **Knowlton**, is in the south and has the nickname the Knamptons (a play

on the Hamptons) for the swanky **19th-century country houses**, owned by Montréalers who use the town as a summer getaway. It's worth driving off the main road for a peek at the architectural heritage.

The Drive » On the 43km drive from Knowlton, Lac Brome, to Magog, you'll first pass the Abbaye St-Benoît-du-Lac. Take Rte 243 east for five minutes and the left turnoff at Chemin de

NATIONAL PARKS

There are four national parks in the Eastern Townships, each with a slightly different flavour and all worth making extended stops.

Plan Your Trip

If you plan to camp or stay in a hut, check ahead; some accommodations are quite basic and not all parks are open year-round. The trails leading to the national parks are gravel, so plan for your wheels to rough it a little.

Parc National du Mont Orford

Compact Park National de Mont Orford (p96) is a delight in summer and a favorite with families for its gentle hiking trails, kayaking and canoeing in its lakes, and its small size, all conveniently sited 8km northwest from Magog.

Parc National du Mont-Mégantic

The standout feature in this **park** (☎819-888-2941; www.sepaq.com/pq/mme; 189 Rte du Parc; adult/child $8.75/free; ℗♿) at the eastern extremity of the townships 80km east of Sherbrooke is the **AstroLab** (☎819-888-2941; http://astrolab-parc-national-mont-megantic.org/en; 189 Rte du Parc, Notre-Dame-des-Bois; adult/child $19.25/free, Astronomy Evenings $25.25/free; ◷10am-4.30pm & 8pm-late Jun-Aug, check website for other times) observatory and educational center. If you have kids in tow, finish the day's road trip with an astronomy tour (reservations required).

Parc National de la Yamaska

At the heart of this 12-sq-km park near Bromont is an arrow-shaped lake ringed by towering forests. Come here in warm weather to rent sailboards, canoes and rowboats and then stay in a comfortable nature cabin. Visit in winter for snowshoeing and Nordic skiing.

Parc National de Frontenac

Wildlife lovers should make the trek 100km northeast of Sherbrooke to Frontenac to spot more than 200 species of bird and 30 of mammal. The park borders **Lac St-François**, with lakeside campsites and cabins, and has good family water activities as well as hiking and cycling.

DETOUR: COATICOOK

Start: **5** North Hatley

Cheese lovers will find the cheese map provided by the tourism office enough reason to detour to attractive Coaticook, a southern town of the Eastern Townships full of nature activities. The town's big magnet for outdoorsy types is the lush **Parc de la Gorge de Coaticook** (📞819-849-2331; www.gorgedecoaticook.qc.ca; 400 Rue St-Marc, Coaticook; adult/child $7.50/4.50; 🕐information desk 9am-5pm; 🚻) where you can explore the endless green space bordering the USA while riding horseback, mountain biking or hiking. If you have kids (or you are a big kid at heart), aim to visit on a summer evening for one of the highlights of Coaticook, **Foresta Lumina** (📞819-849-2331; www.forestalumina.com; 135 Rue Michaud, Coaticook; adult/child $19.50/11.50; 🕐8:30-10:30pm Jul & Aug, Fri & Sat Jun, Sep & early Oct; 🚻), an outdoor light show where forest trails turn into colorful lit-up paths through the national park. At other times, there is an animal petting farm, and winter snow-tubing. Be sure to stop off for a maple-syrup ice cream at **Laiterie De Coaticook Ltée** at 1000 Rue Child. From North Hatley head east on Rte 143 and then south along Rte 147 for 28km (30 minutes) to Parc de la Gorge de Coaticook. To rejoin the main part of the trip, head north on Rte 147, becoming Rte 143, for 33km (30 minutes) straight to Sherbrooke.

Glen, passing picturesque ponds and some unpaved roads to the abbey after 23km. Then follow the lakeside road north 20km to Magog.

---

4 Magog (p96)

Just 20km before you enter Magog from the south, the **Ab-baye St-Benoît-du-Lac** (📞819-843-4080; www. abbaye.ca; 1 Rue Principale, St-Benoît-du-Lac; 🕐 church 5am-8:30pm, shop 9-10:45am & 11:45am-6pm Mon-Sat) is an unmissable highlight of the townships. The complex mixes tradi-tional architecture, such as a tall church tower, with modern features, such as colorful tiling. The abbey is framed by the wide, dark expanse of Lac Memphrémagog.

The forested moun-tains, are particularly spectacular in the fall or dressed in winter snow. A visit is especially magi-cal if you can coincide with the thrice-daily Gregorian chanting recit-als. Drop by the abbey to buy products made by monks, such as blueber-ries dipped in choco-late, cider and cheese. Continue on with a drive through pretty down-town Magog and around Lac Memphrémagog to ogle the waterfront prop-erties. You can even take a narrated boat cruise on the lake, if you have extra time up your sleeve and book a month in ad-vance. The **Parc National du Mont Orford** (📞819-843-9855; www.sepaq.com/

pq/mor; 3321 Chemin du Parc, Orford; adult/child $8.75/free, parking $8.50; [P] 🚻) is also nearby for winter skiing and summer hiking.

The Drive ›› The short but hilly 18km drive east from Magog to North Hatley passes by impressive red-brick stately houses in the loftiest section and then the road narrows and becomes surrounded by thick trees just before North Hatley. If you can make it to North Hatley's Farmers Markets, enter by car along Capelton and park for free.

---

5 North Hatley (p97)

North Hatley is what first-timers to the region picture as the Eastern Townships and it is this beauty, easily one of the top stunners in

WHY THIS IS A CLASSIC TRIP
PHILLIP TANG,
WRITER

This trip takes you into the heart of classic, slow Québécois life with wholesome, locally produced food. Many think that an abbey sounds like a dressed-up church, until they reach Abbaye St-Benoît-du-Lac and get to taste cheese and cider made by monks, who then break into Gregorian chanting. All this plus knock-out lakes and mountains once you continue on your merry way.

Above: Parc National du Mont Orford (p39)
Left: Historic inn, North Hatley (p39)
Right: Abbaye St-Benoît-du-Lac (p39)

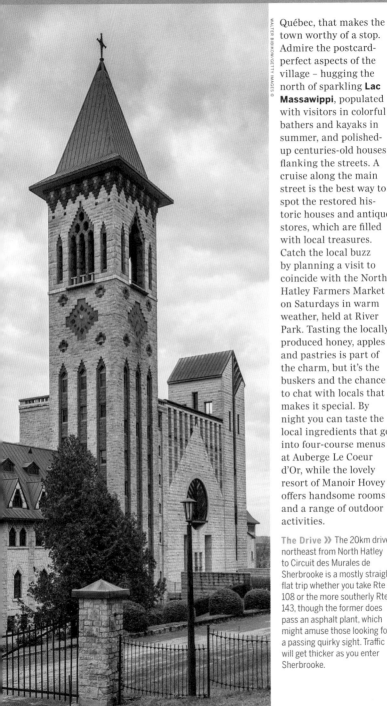

Québec, that makes the town worthy of a stop. Admire the postcard-perfect aspects of the village – hugging the north of sparkling **Lac Massawippi**, populated with visitors in colorful bathers and kayaks in summer, and polished-up centuries-old houses flanking the streets. A cruise along the main street is the best way to spot the restored historic houses and antique stores, which are filled with local treasures. Catch the local buzz by planning a visit to coincide with the North Hatley Farmers Market on Saturdays in warm weather, held at River Park. Tasting the locally produced honey, apples and pastries is part of the charm, but it's the buskers and the chance to chat with locals that makes it special. By night you can taste the local ingredients that go into four-course menus at Auberge Le Coeur d'Or, while the lovely resort of Manoir Hovey offers handsome rooms and a range of outdoor activities.

The Drive ≫ The 20km drive northeast from North Hatley to Circuit des Murales de Sherbrooke is a mostly straight, flat trip whether you take Rte 108 or the more southerly Rte 143, though the former does pass an asphalt plant, which might amuse those looking for a passing quirky sight. Traffic will get thicker as you enter Sherbrooke.

⑥ Sherbrooke (p97)

More of a small city than a township, there are unusual but worthy attractions to make Sherbrooke, the last of the main Eastern Townships, your final destination for this trip. Hunt for the 11 **street murals** dotted downtown at the **Circuit des Murales de Sherbrooke** starting from the corner of Rue Frontenac and Wellington. Each piece tells a local story of the people and region, including painted life-size re-creations of shop facades that once stood in the area. From a distance, the facades are camouflaged by the adjacent real stores, adding to the hunt-and-discovery fun, especially for tired kids at the end of a road trip. At **Bishop's University** (www.ubishops.ca/st-marks-chapel; Rue du Collège, Lennoxville) original architecture abounds, with most of the two-dozen buildings dating from the 1840s. The most conventionally attractive architectural sight is St Mark's Chapel, which woos visitors with stained-glass windows and decorative pews.

Rivière St-François, Sherbrooke
WALTER BIBIKOW/GETTY IMAGES ©

Around, Over & In the St Lawrence River

With an island that's a locavore's paradise, waterfalls in spades, Québec's most sacred church, artsy towns and the St Lawrence River forever in view... What's not to love?

4

TRIP HIGHLIGHTS

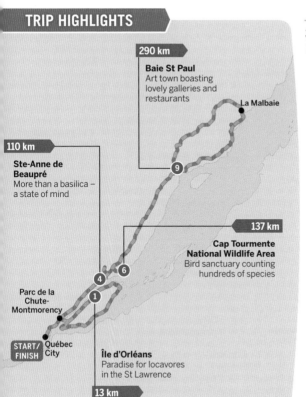

290 km

Baie St Paul
Art town boasting lovely galleries and restaurants

La Malbaie

110 km

Ste-Anne de Beaupré
More than a basilica – a state of mind

⑨

137 km

Cap Tourmente National Wildlife Area
Bird sanctuary counting hundreds of species

④ ⑥

Parc de la Chute-Montmorency

①

START/FINISH Québec City

Île d'Orléans
Paradise for locavores in the St Lawrence

13 km

**3 DAYS
383KM/238 MILES**

GREAT FOR...

BEST TIME TO GO
Visit May/June for springtime flowers and produce, September/October for magical fall colors.

ESSENTIAL PHOTO
La mer (the sea) that is the St Lawrence River from La Malbaie.

BEST FOR CULTURE
Baie St Paul is a food and arts hub.

Around, Over & In the St Lawrence River

4

This drive, with the St Lawrence River at its heart, will circle you around idyllic Île d'Orléans, an island dotted with strawberry fields, apple orchards, windmills, workshops and galleries, across to the Côte de Beaupré, with a waterfall taller than Niagara Falls and Québec's largest basilica, and on to Charlevoix, a stunning outdoors playground with some lovely local towns crammed with artists' studios, galleries and boutiques.

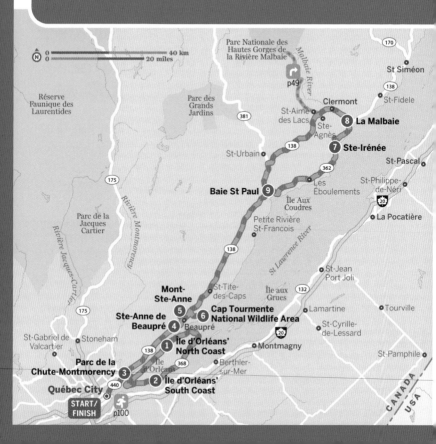

N
0 _____ 40 km
0 _____ 20 miles

Parc Nationale des Hautes Gorges de la Rivière Malbaie

p49

170
St Siméon

138
St-Fidèle

Réserve Faunique des Laurentides

Parc des Grands Jardins

381

Clermont

St-Aimé-des-Lacs

8 La Malbaie

Ste-Agnès

7 Ste-Irénée

138

St-Urbain

362

St-Pascal

Les Éboulements

St-Philippe-de-Néri

20

Baie St Paul 9

Île Aux Coudres

La Pocatière

175

Petite Rivière St-Francois

Parc de la Jacques Cartier

138

Rivière Jacques-Cartier

Rivière Montmorency

St-Jean Port Joli

Mont-Ste-Anne

St-Tite-des-Caps

Île aux Grues

132

Lamartine

Tourville

175

5

6 Cap Tourmente National Wildlife Area

Ste-Anne de Beaupré 4

Beaupré

St-Cyrille-de-Lessard

St-Pamphile

St-Gabriel de Valcartier

Stoneham

20

Montmagny

138

1 Île d'Orléans' North Coast

Parc de la Chute-Montmorency 3

Île d'Orléans

368

Berthier-sur-Mer

St-Pamphile

Québec City

2 Île d'Orléans' South Coast

START/FINISH

p100

CANADA
USA

❶ Île d'Orléans' North Coast (p105)

'Orléans Island,' 15km northeast of Québec City, with a population of just 6825, is still primarily a farming region and has emerged as the epicenter of Québec's agritourism movement. Foodies from all around flock to the local *économusées* (workshops) to watch culinary artisans at work.

To reach the island from Québec City, take Rte 440 Est to the Pont de l'Île d'Orléans, the huge suspension bridge leading to the island, then join Rte 368. This 60km-long road encircles the island, with two more cutting across it north–south.

There are a half-dozen villages on the island. On the north side you'll find St-Pierre, Ste-Famille and St-François, each with its own attractions. Before setting out, though, stop in at the **Île d'Orléans tourist office** (☎866-941-9411, 418-828-9411; http://tourisme.iledorleans. com/en; 490 Côte du Pont, St-Pierre; ⏰8:30am-6pm early Jun-early Sep, to 4:30pm rest of year), which you'll come to after crossing the bridge. Its very complete *Autour de l'Île d'Orléans* (Around the Île d'Orléans) brochure is well worth the $1 charged for it.

Then make a beeline to any of the many workshops and boutiques lining the road in St-Pierre, including **Cassis Monna & Filles** (www.cassismonna.com/en; 1225 Chemin Royal, St-Pierre; ⏰10am-8pm Jun-Sep, 11:30am-8pm Oct-May), where everything from mustard to liqueur is made from blackcurrants, and **La Nougaterie Québec** (www.nougateriequebec.com; 1367 Chemin Royal, St-Pierre; ⏰10am-5pm Mon-Fri, from 11am Sat & Sun), where egg whites and honey are miraculously turned into nougat.

In Ste-Famille, the main draw is **Maison Drouin** (www.maisondrouin. com; 2958 Chemin Royal, Ste-Famille; adult/child $6/free; ⏰10am-6pm mid-Jun–early Sep, noon-4pm Sat & Sun early Sep–mid-Oct), a house dating back to 1730 that has never been modernized, while in St-François you have to climb the wooden **Observation Tower** (325 Chemin Royal, St-François; ⏰sunrise-sunset) for views over the St Lawrence River and the brooding mountains beyond.

The Drive ≫ Nothing could be easier. Just continue on the only highway on the island – Rte 368 – which loops around the island and back to the bridge (33km).

❷ Île d'Orléans' South Coast (p105)

The next three villages ahead of you on the island's southern coast are St-Jean, St-Laurent and Ste-Pétronille. Their edges are dotted with strawberry fields, orchards, cider producers, windmills, workshops and galleries. Some of the villages contain wooden and stone houses that are up to 300 years old.

If you're feeling peckish, stop off at **La Boulange** (www.laboulange.ca; 4624 Chemin Royal, St-Jean; light meals $5-12; ⏰7:30am-5:30pm Mon-Sat, to 5pm Sun late Jun–early Sep, see website for rest of the year), a memorable bakery and grocery store in St-Jean. Devour to-die-for croissants while taking in views of the St Lawrence and the 18th-century **Église St-Jean** (Church of St John; ☎418-828-2551; 4623 Chemin Royal, St-Jean) next door.

Further along in St-Laurent, the little **Parc Maritime de St-Laurent** (http://parcmaritime.ca/en; 120 Chemin de la Chalouperie, St-Laurent; adult/youth/child $5/3/free; ⏰10am-5pm mid-Jun–mid-Oct; 👣) is worth a look to understand the maritime heritage of the region. At the nearby **La Forge à Pique-Assaut** (www.forge-pique-assaut.com; 2200 Chemin Royal, St-Laurent; ⏰9am-5pm late Jun-early Sep, 9am-noon & 1:30-5pm Mon-Fri mid-Sep–mid-Jun), artisanal blacksmith Guy Bel makes and sells decorative objects at his *économusée*. Our last stop, in Ste-Pétronille, is the incomparable **Chocolaterie de l'Île d'Orléans** (www.chocolaterieorleans. com; 8330 Chemin Royal, Ste-Pétronille; ⏰9.30am-5pm

Mon-Fri, to 6pm Sat & Sun), where *chocolatiers* above a delightful shop in a 200-year-old house churn out tasty concoctions.

The Drive » From Ste-Pétronille's center, continue along Rte 368 and back to the Pont de l'Île d'Orléans. Cross the bridge and join Rte 138 Ouest to the Blvd des Chutes exit and the Parc de la Chute-Montmorency (10km).

- - - - - - - - - - - - - - - - - -

❸ Parc de la Chute-Montmorency

The waterfall in this national park just over the bridge from the Île d'Orléans is 83m high, topping Niagara Falls by about 30m (though it's not nearly as wide). What's cool is walking over the falls on the **suspension bridge** (La Chute-Montmorency) to see (and hear) them thunder down below.

Once you reach the park's entrance you have one of three choices: park the car and take the **cable car** (www.sepaq.com/destinations/parc-chute-montmorency; adult/child one way $12.25/6.30, return $14.35/7.20; ⏰8:30am-7:30pm late Jun–mid-Aug, shorter hours rest of year; Ⓟ 🚻) up to the falls; follow the Promenade de la Chute from the cable car's lower station and climb the 487-step Escalier Panoramique (Panoramic Staircase); or stay in the car and drive to the upper station and the **Manoir**

Montmorency (www.sepaq.com/destinations/parc chute-montmorency; 2490 Ave Royale; ⏰10am-6pm Apr-Oct, to 4pm Nov-Mar), a replica of an 18th-century manor house with an information counter, interpretation center about the falls and park, a shop and a terrace restaurant. To really get the adrenaline going, there's a zip line that shoots across the canyon in front of the falls and three levels of *via ferrata* (climbing trails with fixed ladders and cables).

The Drive » From Parc de la Chute-Montmorency, rejoin Rte 138 and this time travel east. The town and basilica of Ste-Anne de Beaupré are 25km to the northeast.

- - - - - - - - - - - - - - - - - -

❹ Ste-Anne de Beaupré (p107)

The drive along the Côte de Beaupré to the **pilgrimage church** (www.sanctuairesainteanne.org; 10018 Ave Royale; ⏰7am-9:30pm Jun-Aug, 8am-5pm Mon-Sat, to 6pm Sun Sep-May) at Ste-Anne de Beaupré is a delight in any season, including winter, when the ice floes in the St Lawrence shimmer in the sun under the bright blue sky. Approaching along Rte 138, the basilica tower's twin steeples dwarf everything else in town. Since the mid-1600s, the village has been an important Christian site; the annual pilgrimage

around the feast day of St Anne (July 26) draws thousands of visitors. The awe-inspiring basilica you see today was constructed after a devastating blaze in 1922 and has been open since 1934. Inside, don't miss the lovely modern stained-glass windows (there are 214 of them), the impressive tilework and glittering ceiling mosaics depicting the life of St Anne.

A delightful spot to stop for lunch en route to the church is **Auberge Baker** (www.auberge baker.com; 8790 Ave Royale, Château-Richer; mains $22-36; ⏰noon-2pm & 5-8:30pm). It's 5km to the southwest in Château-Richer on Rte 360, which runs parallel inland to Rte 138.

The Drive » Follow Rte 138 Est (also known as Blvd Ste-Anne in these parts) to the fork in the village of Beaupré and join the 360 Est (Ave Royale) to Mont-Ste-Anne.

- - - - - - - - - - - - - - - - - -

❺ Mont-Ste-Anne

This immensely popular **ski resort** (www.mont-sainte-anne.com; 2000 Blvd du Beau-Pré, Beau-Pré; lift ticket adult/youth/child full day $83/57/40, half-day $58/46/30; ⏰8:30am-4pm mid-Dec–Apr; 🚻) is just 50km northeast of Québec City so it gets a lot of weekend skiers, especially between mid-December and well into April. It counts nine lifts and 71 ski trails, nine of which are set aside for

DETOUR:
PARC NATIONAL DES HAUTES GORGES DE LA RIVIÈRE MALBAIE

Start: 8 La Malbaie

This 225-sq-km **provincial park** (📞800-665-6527, 418-439-1227; www.sepaq.com/pq/hgo; 25 Blvd Notre-Dame, Clermont; adult/child $8.75/free; 🕐visitor center 9am-8pm mid-Jun–early Sep; 🅿🐾) has several unique features, including the highest rock faces east of the Rockies. Sheer rock plummets (by as much as 800m) to the calm Malbaie River, creating one of Québec's loveliest river valleys.

There are trails of all levels, from ambles around the 2.5km loop of the L'Érablière (Maple Grove) to vigorous hikes of up to 11km ascending to permafrost. A highlight is the boat cruise up the river, squeezed between mountains. The river can also be seen from a canoe or kayak, which are available for hire, as are mountain bikes. Boat tickets and rentals are available at the Le Draveur Visitor Center at the park entrance. The park is located about 40km northwest of La Malbaie. To reach it, head northwest on Rte 138 toward Baie St Paul, then take the turn for St-Aimé des Lacs and keep going for another 30km.

---

night skiing (from 4pm to 9pm). You'll find all sorts of other winter activities here, including cross-country skiing, snowshoeing, skating, ice canyoning and dogsledding. You can rent skis and snowboards too.

During the summer, the resort features mountain biking, hiking and golfing opportunities. This is also the time to hike to **Jean Larose Waterfalls** (Chutes Jean Larose; 2000 Blvd du Beau-Pré; adult/child $7.80/5.50; 🕐9am-4pm May-Oct) in a deep chasm to the south across Rte 360. With a drop height of 68m, it is one of the most beautiful (and least developed) waterfalls in Québec. You can walk around and across the falls via a series of steps (all 400 of them), ledges and bridges.

The Drive » From Mont-Ste-Anne, follow Rte 360 Ouest (Blvd Beaupré) back to Rte 138 Est and exit at the signposted Chemin du Cap Tourmente (15km).

---

6 Cap Tourmente National Wildlife Area

Lying at the confluence of the upper and lower estuaries of the St Lawrence River, this **wildlife sanctuary** (Réserve Nationale de Faune du Cap-Tourmente; 📞418-827-4591; www.canada.ca/en/environment-climate-change/services/national-wildlife-areas/locations/cap-tourmente.html; 570 Chemin du Cap Tourmente, St-Joachim; adult/youth/child under 12yr $6/5/free; 🕐8:30am-5pm mid-Apr–Oct, to 4pm early Jan–mid-Apr; 🅿) offers contrasting landscapes shaped by the meeting of the river, large coastal marshes, plains and mountains.

It shelters a multitude of habitats that are home to a very wide diversity of animal and plant species. The wildlife area features more than 180 bird species, including flocks of snow geese that migrate to wetlands in spring and autumn. Many of these species are at risk, including the peregrine falcon, the bobolink and the butternut. In addition, there are 30 mammal species, 22 types of forest stands and 700 plant species. The sanctuary is beyond the villages of St-Joachim and Cap-Tourmente; there's a visitor center here and a network of marked trails.

The Drive » Follow the Chemin du Cap Tourmente back up to Rte 138 Est. At Baie St Paul you have a choice, but we recommend following the Uoute du Fleuve along Rte 362

WHY THIS IS A CLASSIC TRIP
STEVE FALLON, WRITER

This drive will introduce you to the best Québec has to offer: the agricultural delights and *économusées* (workshops) of the Île d'Orléans where artisans make everything from cider to nougat; the grandeur of Montmorency Falls; the awesomeness and spirituality of Ste-Anne de Beaupré; and the unspoiled beauty of Charlevoix with its pretty and very arty towns boasting a wide assortment of boutiques, galleries, cafes and restaurants.

Above: Basilica of Ste-Anne de Beaupré (p48)
Left: Montmorency Falls (p48)
Right: Rue St-Jean-Baptiste, Baie St Paul (p52)

MPICELLY/SHUTTERSTOCK ©

Est to Ste-Irénée (88km) and La Malbaie (108km). On the way back you can drive the ear-popping hills of the Route des Montagnes along Rte 138 Ouest.

----

❼ Ste-Irénée

This stretch of the drive is particularly beautiful, with breathtaking views of the St Lawrence as you ride up and down the hills. The first major village is **Les Éboulements**, 'one of the prettiest villages in Québec,' the road signs tell us, with wonderful old wooden houses, an old mill and grazing sheep. Next up is Ste-Irénée, with full-frontal views of the river and its hilltop **Domaine Forget** (☏888-336-7438, 418-452-8111; www.domaine forget.com; 5 Rang St-Antoine), a music and dance academy with a 600-seat hall that attracts classical and jazz musicians and dancers from around the world, particularly during its annual festival in summer. Just down the hill from the village as you approach La Malbaie is the **Observatoire de l'Astroblème de Charlevoix** (www.astrobleme charlevoix.org; 595 Côte Bellevue, Pointe-au-Pic; 1/2/3 activities adult $14/26/36, child $7/13/18; ⊙10am-5pm late Jun-early Sep, to 9pm when cloudy; ♿), an observatory that examines how meteors created the valleys on which Charlevoix sits through multimedia exhibits.

The Drive » It's just 20km along Rte 362 Est to La Malbaie from Ste-Irénée.

----

❽ La Malbaie (p108)

La Malbaie is a town on the St Lawrence River at the mouth of the Malbaie River. The river's so wide here that locals call it *la mer* (the sea). Formerly Murray Bay, the town actually encompasses five once-distinct villages. The first you'll encounter along Rte 362 Est from Ste-Irénée is Pointe-au-Pic, a holiday destination for the wealthy at the beginning of the 20th century and Canada's first seaside resort. To learn more about the town's history, visit the **Musée de Charlevoix** (www.museedecharle voix.qc.ca; 10 Chemin du Havre, Pointe-au-Pic; adult/child $8/6; ⊘9am-5pm Jun–mid-Oct, 10am-5pm Mon-Fri, 1-5pm Sat & Sun mid-Oct–May; 🚸). It's right on the water so you'll get some lovely views of 'the sea.' For more dramatic ones, head up to the **Auberge des 3**

Canards (www.auberge3 canards.com; 115 Côte Bellevue, Pointe-au-Pic) for lunch or tea and take a seat on the sprawling verandah. It's not far from the **Fairmont Le Manoir Richelieu** (www.fairmont.com/richelieu-charlevoix; 181 Rue Richelieu, Pointe-au-Pic), sister hotel to Québec City's Fairmont Le Château Frontenac (p98), with almost as much history and prestige: it dates to 1899.

The Drive » For a little variety, take the Route des Montagnes (Mountain Route) along Rte 138 Ouest to Baie St Paul (49km).

----

❾ Baie St Paul (p107)

Arguably the most interesting of all the little towns along the St Lawrence, this unique blend of the outdoors and the bohemian – Cirque du Soleil originated here – may be the most attractive. Plan to kick off your shoes and stay awhile and, if you do overnight, book the delightful Auberge à l'Ancrage and have a meal at either the Alsatian Le Diapason or

the very French **Le Mouton Noir** (www.moutonnoir-resto.com; 43 Rue Ste-Anne; set meals $37-43; ⊘11am-3pm & 5-11pm, evenings only Wed-Sun winter). The architecturally arresting **Musée d'Art Contemporain de Baie St Paul** (www.macbsp. com; 23 Rue Ambroise-Fafard; adult/student/child $10/7/free; ⊘10am-5pm mid-Jun–Aug, 11am-5pm Tue-Sun Sep–mid-Jun), with contemporary art by local artists and some photographic exhibits from its own collection of 3000 pieces, makes a valiant (but not entirely successful) effort to present the town as an artistic hub. Instead, visit one of the local galleries such as the **Galerie d'Art Beauchamp** (www.galeriebeauchamp. com; 16 Rue St-Jean-Baptiste; ⊘9:30am-5:30pm) just up from the helpful **Baie St Paul Tourist Office** (www. tourisme-charlevoix.com; 6 Rue St-Jean-Baptiste; ⊘9am-6pm May-Sep, to 4pm Oct-Apr).

The Drive » From Baie St Paul you can return to Québec City via Rte 138 Ouest (95km) and walk around the Old Town's historical buildings and museums.

Destinations

Ontario (p56)

From the foodies, fashionistas and funsters of multicultural Toronto to dazzling shorelines and natural wonders, Ontario will have you captivated.

Québec (p84)

A bastion of Francophone identity, Québec offers an interplay of vast wilderness and cosmopolitanism, including stellar gastronomy.

Rue du Petit-Champlain, Québec City (p98)
ANDRIY BLOKHIN/SHUTTERSTOCK ©

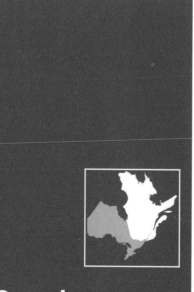

The breathtaking four-seasonal palette of Ontario's vast wilderness, endless forests and abundant wildlife awaits. Let Ontario surprise you with the beauty of its scenery and welcome you with the warmth of its people.

Ontario

TORONTO

POP 5.9 MILLION

Where to begin? Toronto is itself a cultural phenomenon, with residents from around the world and scores of languages, foods, customs and celebrations – they're what make the city great. As Canada's largest city, Toronto has outstanding museums and galleries, from the Frank Gehry–redesigned Art Gallery of Ontario to the delightful Bata Shoe Museum (yes, shoes). The same goes for theaters; the gorgeous Elgin & Winter Garden Theatre has backstage tours as well as regular shows, and Shakespeare in High Park every summer. Then there's live music, poetry readings, comedy shows and LGBTIQ+ spots, too. But nowhere is Toronto's remarkable diversity more evident than in its food and restaurants. There's Pakistani, Persian and Portuguese; indigenous and new fusion; Japanese pancakes and Korean barbecue; and fresh pasta in Little Italy, shawarmas in Greektown and the best damn dumplings in Chinatown. You'll find all walks of life and all colors, flavors and traditions of the world represented here.

◎ Sights

Downtown Toronto is an easy-to-navigate grid bounded by a hodgepodge of bohemian, cultural and historic neighborhoods. Yonge St, the world's longest thoroughfare, dissects the city: an East or West designation indicates a street's position relative to Yonge.

Most sights are found in the Waterfront, Entertainment and Financial Districts at the southern end of downtown. Just north, Yorkville and the Annex have a cache of museums. Due south, locals retreat to the Toronto Islands for beaches and hands-down the best skyline views.

Back on the mainland, the pocket between Yonge and the Don Valley Pkwy enfolds some of Toronto's oldest and best-preserved neighborhoods: St Lawrence Market, the Distillery District and Cabbagetown. Many argue that West is best: Kensington Market and Queen West are edgy and artsy. Meanwhile, the East is full of flavor: Leslieville, Greektown and the Beaches, which are ever so slightly San Franciscan in their outlook and sensibilities, represent the main draws.

★ Harbourfront Centre   ARTS CENTER
(☑ 416-973-4000; www.harbourfrontcentre.com; 235 Queens Quay W; ⊙ 10am-11pm Mon-Sat, to 9pm Sun; P ⋔; 🚋 509, 510) An artistic powerhouse, this 4-hectare complex educates and entertains Toronto's community through a variety of year-round performances, events and exhibits. The center is made up of more than two dozen waterfront venues, including parks, outdoor stages, theaters and galleries. The main building alone houses the well-respected Craft & Design Studios, open studios where the public can watch artists-in-residence at work; the 1300-seat Concert Stage; and even a lakeside rink (p62) where you can slice up the winter ice.

★ CN Tower   TOWER
(La Tour CN; ☑ 416-868-6937; www.cntower.ca; 301 Front St W; Tower Experience adult/child $38/28; ⊙ 8:30am-11pm; ⋔; 🚇 Union) Toronto's iconic CN Tower, a communications spire and a marvel of 1970s engineering, looks like a giant concrete hypodermic needle. Riding one of the glass elevators up what was once the world's highest freestanding structure (553m) is one of those things you just *have* to do in Toronto. Even if you don't, you're bound to catch a glimpse of the tower at night: the entire structure puts on a brilliant (free) light show year-round.

★ 401 Richmond   GALLERY
(☑ 416-595-5900; www.401richmond.com; 401 Richmond St W; ⊙ 9am-7pm Mon-Fri, to 6pm Sat; 🚋 510) **FREE** Inside an early-20th-century lithographer's warehouse, restored in 1994, this 18,500-sq-meter New York–style artists collective hums with the creative vibes of more than 140 contemporary galleries, exhibition spaces, studios and shops representing works in almost any medium you can think of. Speaker series and film fests are held throughout the year. Grab a snack at the ground-floor cafe (open 9am to 5pm Monday to Friday) and enjoy it on the expansive roof garden, a little-known oasis in summer.

★ Ripley's Aquarium of Canada   AQUARIUM
(☑ 647-351-3474; www.ripleysaquariumofcanada.com; 288 Bremner Blvd; adult/child $32/22; ⊙ 9am-11pm; ⋔; 🚇 Union) Arguably one of Toronto's best attractions for both young and old, it has more than 16,000 aquatic animals and 5.7 million liters of water in the combined tanks. There are touch tanks, a glass tunnel with a moving walkway, educational dive

presentations...and even live jazz on the second Friday of each month. Open 365 days a year. Peak hours are 11am to 4pm.

★ Hockey Hall of Fame   MUSEUM
(☑ 416-360-7765; www.hhof.com; Brookfield Place, 30 Yonge St; adult/child $20/14; ⊙ 9:30am-6pm Mon-Sat, 10am-6pm Sun Jun-Sep, 10am-5pm Mon-Fri, 9:30am-6pm Sat, 10:30am-5pm Sun Oct-May; ⋔; 🚇 Union) Inside the rococo gray-stone Bank of Montreal building (c 1885), the Hockey Hall of Fame is a Canadian institution. Even those unfamiliar with the rough, super-fast sport are likely to be impressed by this, the world's largest collection of hockey memorabilia. Check out the *Texas Chainsaw Massacre*–esque goalkeeping masks or go head to head with the great Wayne Gretzky, virtual-reality style. And, of course, be sure to take a pic with the beloved Stanley Cup.

★ St Lawrence Market Complex   MARKET
(☑ 416-392-7219; www.stlawrencemarket.com; 92-95 Front St E; ⊙ 8am-6pm Tue-Thu, to 7pm Fri, 5am-5pm Sat; P; 🚋 503, 504) Old York's sensational St Lawrence Market has been a neighborhood meeting place for over two centuries. The restored, high-trussed 1845 South Market houses more than 120 specialty food stalls and shops: cheese vendors, fishmongers, butchers, bakers and pasta makers. The Carousel Bakery is famed for its peameal-bacon sandwiches and St Urbain for its authentic Montréal-style bagels.

★ Distillery District   AREA
(☑ 416-364-1177; www.thedistillerydistrict.com; 9 Trinity St; ⊙ 10am-7pm Mon-Wed, to 8pm Thu-Sat, 11am-6pm Sun; 🚋 72, 🚋 503, 504) Centered on the 1832 Gooderham and Worts distillery – once the British Empire's largest – the 5-hectare Distillery District is one of Toronto's best downtown attractions. Its Victorian industrial warehouses have been converted into soaring galleries, artists studios, design boutiques, cafes and eateries. On weekends newlyweds pose before a backdrop of red brick and cobblestone, young families walk their dogs and the fashionable shop for art beneath charmingly decrepit gables and gantries. In summer expect live jazz, activities, exhibitions and foodie events.

★ Tommy Thompson Park   PARK
(☑ 416-661-6600; www.tommythompsonpark.ca; Leslie St; ⊙ 4-9pm Mon-Fri, 5:30am-9pm Sat & Sun; 🚋 83 Jones S, 🚋 501) A 5km-long artificial peninsula between the Harbourfront and the Beaches, Tommy Thompson Park reaches

Toronto

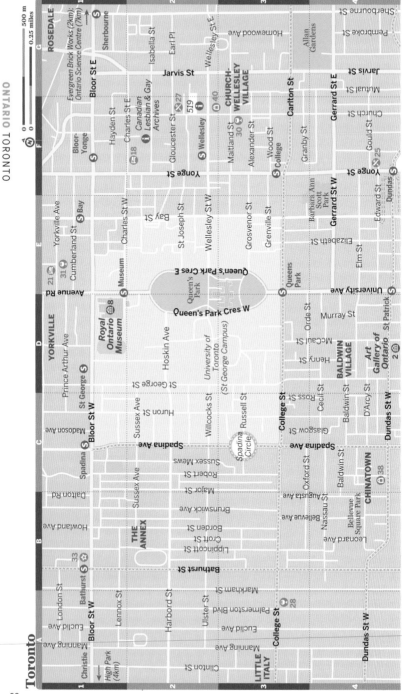

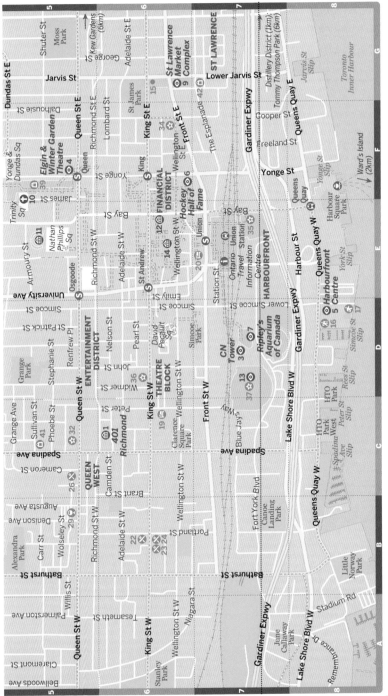

Bellwoods Ave
Claremont St
Palmerston Ave
Wilis St
Tecumseth St
Cameron St
Grange Ave
Sullivan St
Phoebe St
Stephanie St
Renfrew Pl
St Patrick St
Simcoe St
University Ave
Armoury St
Trinity Sq
Yonge & Dundas Sq
Shuter St
Moss Park

Queen St W
Dundas St E
Dalhousie St
Jarvis St

Alexandra Park
Carr St
Wolseley St

QUEEN WEST
Camden St
Brant St

Denison Ave
Augusta Ave

26
29

Richmond St W
Adelaide St W
22
23 24

Portland St

1 401 Richmond
32
41

Spadina Ave

ENTERTAINMENT DISTRICT
Nelson St
Pearl St
David Pecault Sq
John St
Widmer St 36
Peter St

THEATRE BLOCK
King St W 19

Clarence Square Park
Wellington St W
Front St W

Simcoe Park

37 13

CN Tower 3
Ripley's Aquarium of Canada 7

Queen St E
Osgoode
11
Nathan Phillips Sq
Elgin & Winter Garden Theatre 4
Richmond St E
Lombard St

Queen St E
St James Park
Richmond St E

Adelaide St E
George St
Kew Gardens (5km)

Dundas St E

10
39
James St

Bay St
Adelaide St W
St Andrew
14
12
Wellington St W
20
Union
St
Yonge St

King St E 34
King St

FINANCIAL DISTRICT 6
Hockey Hall of Fame
King St E
Wellington St E
Front St E

St Lawrence Market 9
St LAWRENCE COMPLEX
15
Lower Jarvis St

Jarvis St Ship
Toronto Inner Harbour

Distillery District (1km); Tommy Thompson Park (6km)
Cooper St
Queens Quay E
Freeland St

The Esplanade 42
Gardiner Expwy

Yonge St

Ward's Island (2km)
Yonge St Slip
Harbour Square Park

Emily St
Station St
Ontario Travel Information Centre
Union Station 1
35
Lower Simcoe St

HARBOURFRONT
Harbour St
Queens Quay W
Queens Quay

Blue Jays Way
Fort York Blvd
Canoe Landing Park
Spadina Ave

HTO Park West
Spadina Ave Slip
Peter St Slip
Rees St
Simcoe St Slip
York St Slip

16
Harbourfront Centre 5
17

Bathurst St
Little Norway Park
Stanley Park
King St W
Wellington St W
Niagara St

June Callaway Park
Remembrance Dr
Stadium Rd

Gardiner Expwy
Lake Shore Blvd W
Queens Quay W
Lake Shore Blvd W

59

Toronto

further into Lake Ontario than the Toronto Islands. This 'accidental wilderness' – constructed from Outer Harbour dredgings – has become a phenomenal wildlife success. It's one of the world's largest nesting places for ring-billed gulls, and is a haven for terns, black-crowned night herons, turtles, owls, foxes and even coyotes.

★**Elgin & Winter Garden Theatre**   THEATER
(☎416-314-2871; www.heritagetrust.on.ca/ewg; 189 Yonge St; tours adult/student $12/10; Ⓢ Queen) This restored masterpiece is the world's last operating Edwardian double-decker theater. Celebrating its centennial in 2013, the Winter Garden was built as the flagship for a vaudeville chain that never really took off, while the downstairs Elgin was converted into a movie house in the 1920s. Today it serves as a stage for traveling Broadway shows. Fascinating tours run at 5pm Monday and 10am Saturday.

★Art Gallery of Ontario   GALLERY
(AGO; ☎416-979-6648; www.ago.net; 317 Dundas St W; adult/under 25yr $25/free, 6-9pm Wed free; ☺10:30am-5pm Tue & Thu, to 9pm Wed & Fri, to 5:30pm Sat & Sun; 🚍505) The AGO houses collections both excellent and extensive (bring your stamina). Renovations of the facade, designed by the revered Frank Gehry and completed in 2008, impress at street level: it's like looking at a huge crystal ship docked on a city street. Inside, highlights of the collection include rare Québecois religious statuary, Inuit carvings, stunningly presented works by Canadian greats the Group of Seven, the Henry Moore sculpture pavilion, and restored Georgian house The Grange.

★**Royal Ontario Museum**   MUSEUM
(ROM; ☎416-586-8000; www.rom.on.ca; 100 Queen's Park; adult/child $23/14, 5:30-8:30pm 3rd Mon of month free; ☺10am-5:30pm, to 8:30pm 3rd Mon of month; Ⓢ Museum) Opened in 1914, the multidisciplinary ROM is Canada's biggest natural-history museum and one of the largest museums in North America. You'll either love or loathe the synergy between the original heritage buildings at the main entrance on Bloor St and the 2007 addition of 'the Crystal,' which appears to pierce the original structure and juts out into the street. There are free docent-led tours daily.

High Park   PARK
(www.toronto.ca/parks; 1873 Bloor St W; ☉ dawn-
dusk; P 🚻; S High Park, 🚌 501, 506, 508) Toronto's favorite green space is a wonderful
spot to unfurl a picnic blanket, swim, play
tennis, bike around, skate on 14-hectare
Grenadier Pond or – in spring – meander
through the groves of cherry blossoms
donated by the Japanese ambassador in
1959. Several nature walks, workshops and
various talks are organized by the Nature
Centre (https://highparknaturecentre.com)
and led by rangers.

    Shakespeare in High Park (☎ 416-368-3110;
www.canadianstage.com; High Park, 1873 Bloor St W;
suggested donation adult/child $20/free; ☉ 8pm
Tue-Sun Jul-Sep; S High Park, 🚌 501, 506, 508) has
been produced in the park's amphitheater
for almost 40 years.

Evergreen Brick Works   PARK
(☎ 416-596-7670; www.evergreen.ca; 550 Bayview
Ave; ☉ 9am-5pm Mon-Fri, 8am-5pm Sat, 10am-
5pm Sun; P 🚻; 🚌 28A, S Broadview) 🚲 FREE
Famed for the transformation of its
once-deteriorating heritage buildings into
a prime location for all things geotourism,
this dynamic, LEED-certified environ-
mental center and park hosts interactive
workshops and community festivals on
the themes of ecology, technology and the
environment. There's a garden market, an
ice rink and lots of nature trails, which can
be explored on foot or by bike (rentals are
available).

    Check the website to see what's going on.
Take the free shuttle bus from Broadview
subway station.

McMichael Canadian
Art Collection   GALLERY
(☎ 905-893-1121; www.mcmichael.com; 10365
Islington Ave, Kleinburg; adult/child $18/15, Tue
$15/12; ☉ 10am-5pm May-Oct, to 4pm Tue-Sun Nov-
Apr; P; 🚌 13) Handcrafted buildings (including painter Tom Thomson's cabin, moved
from its original location), set amid 40 hectares of conservation trails, contain works
by Canada's best-known landscape painters,
the Group of Seven, as well as works by First
Nations, Inuit, Métis and other acclaimed
Canadian artists.

    It's a 34km, 45-minute drive from Toron-
to and is totally worth the trip. A sculpture
garden and the graves of gallery co-found-
ers Robert and Signe McMichael and six of
the Group of Seven artists can also be seen
on-site.

◉ Toronto Islands

For independent travelers the Toronto Islands' main sights are the beaches, situat-
ed along the islands' southern, lake-facing
shore. Each beach has its own appeal – family
friendly, less busy and even clothing optional
– though all are worth visiting if you have
the time. The harbor side has no beaches
but terrific views of Toronto's skyline. Travelers with young children will likely want to
visit the amusement park (p68) on Centre
Island.

Ward's Island Beach   BEACH
(☎ beach hotline 416-392-7161; Lakeshore Ave, Ward's
Island; 🚢 Ward's Island) Arguably the prettiest beach on the Toronto Islands, this is a
long, curving shoreline with tawny sand and
views of boats sailing past. Lifeguards are on
duty from 11:30am to 6:30pm daily (May to
September). It's on the south side of Ward's
Island.

⛹ Activities

They're often muffled in winter layers, but
Torontonians still like to keep fit. Outdoor
activities abound: folks walk, cycle and jog
along the lakeshore and hike up the city's ra-
vines. They kayak and paddleboard on Lake
Ontario. Ice-skating and hockey are winter
faves.

Martin Goodman Trail   WALKING
(Queens Quay W) The Martin Goodman Trail,
a 56km path running the length of Toronto's lakeshore, cuts through the Waterfront
neighborhood. The relatively flat path is
mostly paved; it's used by joggers, cyclists
and folks just out for a stroll. From here, the
prettiest direction is east toward the Hum-
ber River Bridge, passing urban parks and
beaches along the way.

Toronto Islands Bicycle Rental   CYCLING
(☎ 416-203-0009; www.torontoislandbicyclerental.
com; Centre Island; per hour bicycles/tandems $9/16,
2-/4-seat quadricycles $18/32; ☉ 11am-5pm May-
Sep; 🚻; 🚢 Centre Island) One of the best ways
to explore the islands is by bike. A variety of
options are offered here, including tandems,
quadricycles and smaller frames for kids.
Helmets are provided. Look for the shop
next to Outlook Pier.

Toronto Island SUP   WATER SPORTS
(☎ 416-899-1668; www.torontoislandsup.com; 13
Algonquin Bridge Rd, Algonquin Island; 2hr tours from
$79, yoga $49, rental 1st/additional hour $30/10;

⊙10:30am-before sunset Mon-Fri, 10am-6pm Sat & Sun; ⊠Ward's Island) 🏄 Join a paddleboard tour to explore the 14 islands that make up the Toronto Islands archipelago. Morning and afternoon excursions focus on flora and fauna, while night tours (with illuminated paddles) let you take in the city views. There are whimsical ukulele tours (yep, paddle and play) and yoga classes on the water, too. Rentals available. Launches are from Algonquin Bridge.

Ice-Skating

Locals love to skate. When the weather's freezing and the snow's falling lightly, downtown Toronto's outdoor ice rinks come alive. The best-known rinks are at Nathan Phillips Square outside City Hall (☑416-392-2489, 311; www.toronto.ca; 100 Queen St W; ⊙8:30am-4:30pm Mon-Fri Nov-Mar; Ⓟ; Ⓢ Queen) FREE and the Natrel Rink (☑416-954-9866; www.harbourfrontcentre.com; Harbourfront Centre, 235 Queens Quay W; ⊙9am-10pm Sun-Thu, to 11pm Fri & Sat Nov-Mar; ♿; 🚋509, 510) FREE at the Harbourfront Centre. These artificial rinks are open daily (weather permitting) from mid-November to March. Admission is free; skate rental is available.

Toronto Parks & Recreation (www.toronto.ca/parks) has info on other rinks around town, including those at Kew Gardens (www.toronto.ca; 2075 Queen St E; ⊙dawn-dusk; ♿; 🚋501) in the Beaches and Trinity Bellwoods Park in the West End. If it's been *really* cold, you can skate on Grenadier Pond in High Park (p61). Beginners might prefer the lesser-known Ryerson Rink, tucked away just north of Yonge & Dundas Sq at 25 Gould St – in summer the rink is a water feature.

☞ Tours

Between May and September cruise operators sail from the waterfront beside Queens Quay Terminal or York Quay Centre. Reservations are recommended for brunch and dinner cruises. Keep in mind that ferries to the Toronto Islands offer similar views for half the price.

★Toronto Bicycle Tours   CYCLING
(☑416-477-2184; https://torontobicycletours.com; adult/child from $75/46; ⊙8am-6pm) Offering year-round bike tours – even in winter (ponchos and gloves provided) – of downtown, 15 neighborhoods and the Toronto Islands. Excursions are for all levels and ages, and last 3½ to seven hours. Bike, helmet, water and snacks are provided (plus a picnic lunch for longer tours). Multilingual guides or interpreters, too.

★Heritage Toronto   WALKING
(☑416-338-3886; www.heritagetoronto.org; 157 King St E; suggested donation $10; ⊙May-Oct) A diverse offering of fascinating historical, cultural and nature walks, as well as bus (TTC) tours, led by museum experts, neighborhood historical-society members and emerging historians. Tours generally last one to three hours. Check the website for a handful of downloadable self-guided tours, too.

✦ Festivals & Events

Hot Docs   FILM
(Canadian International Documentary Festival; tickets from $17.50; ⊙late Apr-early May;) North America's largest documentary-film festival screens more than 200 docos from around the globe from its home at the fantastic Hot Docs Ted Rogers Cinema (Bloor Hot Docs Cinema; ☑416-637-3123; http://hotdocscinema.ca; 506 Bloor St W; Ⓢ Bathurst) plus other venues around town, including museums and theaters.

Dreams Festival   MUSIC
(http://dreamsfestival.ca; Ontario Place, 909 Lake Shore Blvd W; ⊙Jun; 🚋509) A two-day festival that draws more than 25,000 ravers and electronic-music lovers every summer to massive Ontario Place along Toronto's waterfront.

Luminato   CULTURAL
(☑416-368-4849;www.luminatofestival.com;⊙Jun) Luminato seeks to bring a broad selection of the world's most accomplished musicians, dancers, artists, writers, actors and filmmakers to venues across Toronto in a celebration of creativity that reflects the city's diversity. Many performances are free. Past performers have included Aretha Franklin, Joni Mitchell, kd lang and Rufus Wainwright.

Pride Toronto   LGBTIQ+
(☑416-927-7433; www.pridetoronto.com; ⊙Jun) Toronto's most flamboyant event celebrates the diversity of sexuality and gender identity, with a whole month (it was a week) of community events, workshops and gatherings, mostly free. The celebration climaxes with a Trans March, Dyke March and Pride Parade at the end of June, when the streets around Church and Wellesley ('the Village') heave with over a million revelers.

Toronto Fringe Festival
CULTURAL

(☎416-966-1062; http://fringetoronto.com; tickets $13; ⊙early Jul) Celebrating over 30 years in the spotlight, Toronto's largest theater and performance festival hosts more than 150 productions on three dozen stages over two weeks in early July. Ranging from offbeat to seriously emotive and including a program of kids' plays, the festival aims to make theater accessible to all. It's worth booking your trip to Toronto to coincide with it.

Toronto International Film Festival
FILM

(TIFF; ☎888-599-8433; www.tiff.net; ⊙Sep; 📷504) Since its inception in 1976, TIFF has grown to be the crowning jewel of the Toronto festival scene and a key player in the world film circuit. Attracting over 400,000 eager cinephiles to the red-carpet celebrity frenzy of its 10-day run, the festival has become an important forum for showcasing new films.

🛌 Sleeping

Toronto has no shortage of accommodations, from high-rise hotels in the Financial District to boutique hotels in the West End. B&Bs are in residential neighborhoods, while hostels dot the city. Lodging can be expensive, especially in summer, when rooms sell quickly and at a premium. It's essential to book ahead, remembering that 13% tax will be added to the quoted rate. An additional 3% destination tax is sometimes levied, too.

★ Only Backpackers Inn
HOSTEL $

(☎416-463-3249; http://theonlyinn.com; 966 Danforth Ave; dm incl breakfast $28-33, r incl breakfast $82; ❄ @ 🛜; Ⓢ Donlands) There's so much to love about the Only. Inspired by the owner's globetrotting adventures, it's everything you want a hostel to be: clean, cozy, near the subway, and with a laid-back traveler vibe. There are waffles for brekky and two private patios, plus murals everywhere. The downstairs cafe has a large patio and 24 gourmet brews on tap.

★ Anndore House
HOTEL $$

(☎833-745-8370; https://theanndorehouse.com; 15 Charles St E; r from $242; P ❄ 🛜; Ⓢ Bloor-Yonge) A stylish place with 113 rooms, all with exposed-brick walls, art-deco-meets-boho bathrooms, record players and city views. A hotel app allows guests to control their room's temperature and lighting – a nice touch. Downstairs, a labyrinthine restaurant-bar and a street-side patio are great for an afternoon cocktail or snack.

★ Hazelton
BOUTIQUE HOTEL $$$

(☎416-963-6300; www.thehazeltonhotel.com; 118 Yorkville Ave; d from $484; P ❄ 🛜 ☎ ☎; Ⓢ Bay) Competitors in the luxury class have in recent years made it harder for the Hazelton to uphold its self-professed reputation as Toronto's most exclusive hotel: but try it will, and you'll only benefit from its efforts. Sophisticated, dramatic and sexy, this hotel is small enough (with just 62 rooms and 15 suites) to make you feel truly special.

★ Bisha Hotel
BOUTIQUE HOTEL $$$

(☎416-551-2800; www.bishahoteltoronto.com; 80 Blue Jays Way; d from $379; P ❄ ❄ 🛜 ☎; 📷504) Upscale but decently priced Bisha is a luxury hotel and residence in the heart of the Entertainment District; it's also right off King St W, a chic neighborhood lined with popular bars and restaurants. Rooms are sleek and stylish, and there's a rooftop pool with stunning views of Toronto's famous skyline.

🍴 Eating

Nowhere is Toronto's multiculturalism more potent and thrilling than in its restaurants. You'll find everything from Korean walnut cakes and sweat-inducing Thai curries to good ol' Canuck pancakes with peameal bacon and maple syrup. Fusion food is hot: traditional Western recipes spiked with zingy Eastern ingredients. British influences also linger – fizzy lunchtime pints and formal afternoon high teas are much-loved traditions.

★ Forno Cultura
BAKERY $

(☎416-603-8305; www.fornocultura.com; 609 King St W; items from $3; ⊙7:30am-9:30pm Tue-Sat, 8am-6pm Sun; ⚄ 🚲; 📷504, 508) An Italian bakery tucked into a basement-level shop, Forno Cultura offers a full line of bread and pastries made with ingredients imported from Italy – even the flour and butter! The bakery itself is a long room, one side lined with impossible-to-resist goods, the other with a view of bakers doing their thing. Communal tables encourage you to stay, watch and eat.

★ Outdoor Eateries
FOOD TRUCK $

(335 Yonge St; mains from $3; ⊙11am-10:30pm; ⚄; Ⓢ Dundas, College) Food trucks, repurposed shipping containers and plywood sheds make up this outdoor food court at the heart of Yonge St. Short-order cooks prep burritos, Philly cheesesteak subs, crepes, vegan eats and more. Hungry diners (many of them students from Ryerson U) fill the picnic tables in the center courtyard.

STRETCH YOUR LEGS
TORONTO

Start/Finish: Harbourfront Centre

Distance: 4.6km

Duration: 3 hours

A feast for the eyes and belly, a walk through Toronto's bustling Financial and Old Town districts provides insight into the city's present and past, while the Waterfront is all about art and shimmering lake views.

Harbourfront Centre

Set on Lake Ontario, the **Harbourfront Centre** (www.harbourfrontcentre.com; 235 Queens Quay W; ⊙10am-11pm Mon-Sat, to 9pm Sun; P 🚻; 🚋509, 510) is the place to start. A cultural hub, it's an easy place to wander and explore. It has galleries and open artist studios, an outdoor concert stage and even an ice rink. **Boxcar Social** (www.boxcarsocial.ca; mains $12-18; ⊙9am-5pm Mon, to 11pm Tue-Thu, to late Fri, 10am-late Sat, to 8pm Sun; 🛜🍴; 🚋509, 510), an industrial-chic cafe, is a good place to stop for a salad or cappuccino. For more art, head next door to the engaging **Power Plant Contemporary Art Gallery** (www.thepowerplant.org; 231 Queens Quay W; ⊙10am-5pm Tue, Wed & Fri-Sun, to 8pm Thu; P 🚻; 🚋509, 510) – if in doubt, look for its smokestack.

The Walk » Head west on Queens Quay W and take a right on Rees St. At the top of the hill, dogleg east on Bremner Av to the towering CN Tower.

CN Tower

Toronto's iconic **CN Tower** (La Tour CN; www.cntower.ca; 301 Front St W; Tower Experience adult/child $38/28; ⊙8:30am-11pm; 🚻; S Union) is impossible to miss – it dominates the city skyline. Standing 553m tall, it was once the highest freestanding structure in the world. A ride to the top will reveal breathtaking 360-degree views of the city and a glass-bottom floor that will test your backbone. Afterwards, consider popping into **Ripley's Aquarium of Canada** (www.ripleysaquariumofcanada.com; 288 Bremner Blvd; adult/child $32/22; ⊙9am-11pm; 🚻; S Union) next door.

The Walk » Continue north on the pedestrian bridge adjacent to the CN Tower. Take a right on Front St, passing the historic Union Station, Toronto's longtime transportation hub. At Yonge St, take a left.

Hockey Hall of Fame

On the corner sits Canada's mecca to its beloved national sport: the **Hockey Hall of Fame** (www.hhof.com; Brookfield Place, 30 Yonge St; adult/child $20/14; ⊙9:30am-6pm

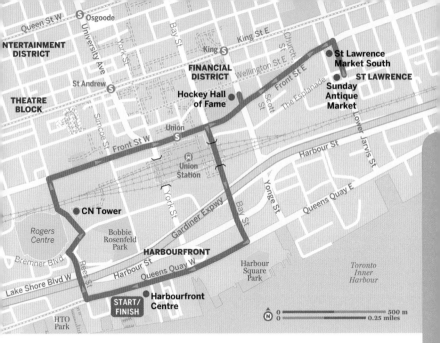

Mon-Sat, 10am-6pm Sun Jun-Sep, 10am-5pm Mon-Fri, 9:30am-6pm Sat, 10:30am-5pm Sun Oct-May; ⛟; ⓢ Union). It's a spectacular tribute to the game, at which visitors learn all about hockey's greats with loads of memorabilia, documentaries and hands-on exhibits such as taking slap shots on simulated NHL goalies or calling a game in a newsroom, teleprompters and all.

The Walk ⟩⟩ Return to Front St and head east, passing the striking Flatiron Building, a favorite of photographers.

St Lawrence Market South

St Lawrence Market (www.stlawrence
market.com; 92-95 Front St E; ⏱8am-6pm Tue-Thu, to 7pm Fri, 5am-5pm Sat; Ⓟ; 🚌503, 504) is the heart of Old Town, a public meeting place since the 1800s. Head inside the Market South building, a beautifully restored complex with more than 120 food stalls and shops selling everything from organic turnips to fresh lake perch. If you're looking for souvenirs, go downstairs to **GiftWorks** (⏱8am-6pm Tue-Thu, to 7pm Fri, 5am-5pm Sat;

🚌503, 504), a little shop packed with quality mementos.

The Walk ⟩⟩ Head back to Front St and take a right on Lower Jarvis St to The Esplanade.

Sunday Antique Market

Directly behind St Lawrence Market South is a huge, semi-permanent tent. On Sundays, you'll find Toronto's **best antique market** (www.facebook.com/
SundayAntiqueMarket; 125 The Esplanade; ⏱7am-4pm Sun; 🚌503, 504) here (the Market North building, its permanent home, is being reconstructed). Rows and rows of vendors sell treasures from the past: tea cups, old photos and leather-bound books. It's a perfect place to wander through, poke around and shop. On Saturdays, the tent transforms into a **Farmers Market**, overflowing with local produce and artisanal goods.

The Walk ⟩⟩ Return to Jarvis St and turn left on Front St, retracing your steps. Take a left on Bay St, admiring the mural of notable indigenous Canadians under the train tracks, circling straight back to Queens Quay W.

★ Parka Food Co. VEGAN $

(☎416-603-3363; www.parkafoodco.com; 424 Queen St W; ☺11:30am-9pm Mon-Thu, to 10pm Fri, noon-10pm Sat, to 8pm Sun; ☝) A starkly white, casual restaurant serving insanely delicious vegan comfort food: burgers made from marinated portobello mushrooms and blackened cauliflower; mac 'n' (vegan) cheese with toppings like truffle mushroom and garlic and onion and thick, flavorful soups. Everything's made in-house from scratch, using locally sourced ingredients.

★ Smith CANADIAN $$

(☎416-926-2501; http://smithrestaurant.com; 553 Church St; mains $18-28; ☺11am-4pm & 5-11pm Tue-Thu, to midnight Fri, 9am-4pm & 5pm-midnight Sat, 9am-4pm Sun; ☝; Ⓢ Wellesley) Come to this bohemian-chic eatery in the heart of the Village for brunch, when the classics are served with flair: eggs Benedict with leek fondue, a short stack with maple cream cheese and candied lemon, or perhaps a Bloody Mary with a bouquet of bacon on top. Is your mouth watering yet? Bookings recommended.

★ Athens GREEK $$

(☎416-465-4441; https://athensdanforth.ca; 707 Danforth Ave; $8-33; ☺11am-midnight; Ⓢ Donlands) As Greek as Greektown (aka The Danforth), modern and beachy Athens serves traditional dishes made with fresh, local ingredients: grilled calamari, lamb *kefte* (meatballs) and, of course, souvlaki. For a treat, try the moussaka and save room for walnut cake. Service is so friendly it feels like family...diners are even welcome in the kitchen to check out what's cooking!

★ Buca ITALIAN $$$

(☎416-865-1600; www.buca.ca; 604 King St W; mains $17-55; ☺11am-3pm & 5-10pm Mon-Wed, 11am-3pm & 5-11pm Thu & Fri, 5-11pm Sat, 5-10pm Sun; ☒304, 504) A breathtaking basement-level restaurant with exposed-brick walls and a soaring ceiling, Buca serves artisanal Italian fare such as homemade pasta and nose-to-tail-style dishes like *orecchio di maiale* (crispy pigs ears) and *cervello* (lamb's brains wrapped in prosciutto and sage). Ease into the experience with a charcuterie board of house-cured meats, flavorful cheeses and bread knots.

★ Lee ASIAN $$$

(☎416-504-7887; www.susur.com/lee; 601 King St W; mains $16-38; ☺5-10:30pm Sun-Wed, to 11pm Thu, to 11:30pm Fri & Sat; ☝; ☒504, 508) Truly a feast for the senses, dinner at acclaimed *cuisinier* Susur Lee's self-titled flagship is

an experience best shared. Slick servers assist in navigating the artisanal selection of East-meets-West delights: you really want to get the pairings right. It's impossible to adequately convey the dance of flavors, textures and aromas one experiences in the signature Singaporean slaw, with...how many ingredients?!

★ Ruby Watchco CANADIAN $$$

(☎416-465-0100; http://rubywatchco.ca; 730 Queen St E; prix fixe $58; ☺6-10pm Tue-Sat; ☒501, 502, 503) Creative farm-to-table comfort food is the game at this homey restaurant, run by two of Toronto's top chefs. (Chef Lynn even stars on the Food Network hit *Pitchin' In*.) A new menu is presented nightly, always four course, always prix fixe. Expect dishes like fried chicken with rosemary honey and maple barbecue ribs; save room for the artisanal cheeses and decadent desserts.

Reservations recommended.

🍸 Drinking & Nightlife

Toronto's drinking scene embraces everything from sticky-carpet dive bars, cookie-cutter 'Brit' pubs and Yankee-style sports bars to slick martini bars, rooftop patios, sky-high cocktail lounges and an effervescent smattering of LGBTIQ+ hangouts. Thirsty work! Strict bylaws prohibit smoking indoors in public spaces, although some patios are permissive. Taps start flowing around midday and last call hovers between 1am and 2am.

★ O'Grady's PUB

(☎416-323-2822; www.ogradyschurch.com; 517 Church St; ☺11am-2am; Ⓢ Wellesley) Come to this friendly Irish pub on Wednesdays for Dirty Bingo nights, when fabulous drag queens call out numbers and give winners risqué prizes from 9pm to midnight. During the day it's all about the patio – the Village's largest – which fills up as soon as the sun comes out. The kitchen, serving comfort food, stays open late.

★ BarChef COCKTAIL BAR

(☎416-868-4800; www.barcheftoronto.com; 472 Queen St W; ☺6pm-2am; Ⓢ Osgoode) You'll hear 'oohs' and 'aahs' coming from the tables in the intimate near-darkness of this swanky bar as cocktails ($16 to $55) emerge alongside a bonsai tree, or under a bell jar of vanilla and hickory-wood smoke. Beyond novelty, drinks show incredible, enticing complexity

Pride Toronto parade (p62)

without overwhelming some unique flavors – truffle snow, chamomile syrup, cedar air and soil!

★ Oxley   PUB

(☑ 647-348-1300; https://theoxley.com; 121 Yorkville Ave; ⊙ 11:30am-midnight Mon-Wed, to 1am Thu, to 2am Fri, 10am-2am Sat, to midnight Sun; ⓦ; Ⓢ Bay) A first-class British pub, the Oxley is located in a 19th-century row house in the heart of Yorkville. Two floors of leather seating, ornate wallpaper and Victorian-era decor attract business folk and the well-heeled hankering for a 20oz pour of craft beer, a glass of wine or a stiff drink. Classic English fare served, too.

★ Bar Raval   BAR

(☑ 647-344-8001; www.thisisbarraval.com; 505 College St; ⊙ 11am-2am Mon-Fri, 10am-2am Sat & Sun; ⓰ 306, 506) Standing in Bar Raval's magnificent, undulating mahogany interior, inspired by the works of Antoni Gaudí, feels like being surrounded by a set of petrified waves – it's otherworldly. The Basque-inspired *pintxos* menu is the perfect complement to the surroundings: small sharing plates (squid in ink, smoked lamb belly, foie gras) go well with the list of layered cocktails and fine wines.

★ Bellwoods Brewery   BREWERY

(www.bellwoodsbrewery.com; 124 Ossington Ave; ⊙ 2pm-midnight Mon-Wed, to 1am Thu & Fri, noon-1am Sat, to midnight Sun; ⓰ 505) Fresh, urban-chic Bellwoods pours award-winning beers, from pale ales and double IPAs to stouts and wild ales.

With candles lighting up the main room and gallery, the brewery itself is decidedly cool and buzzing with locals. Fancy small plates complement the beers.

★ Gladstone Hotel   BAR

(☑ 416-531-4635; www.gladstonehotel.com; 1214 Queen St W; ⊙ 5pm-late Tue-Sat; ⓰ 501) This historic hotel (d/ste from $270/475; Ⓟ ⊝ ✱ ⓦ) revels in Toronto's avant-garde arts scene. The Gladstone Ballroom sustains offbeat DJs, poetry slams, jazz, book readings, alt-country and blues, and burlesque, while the Melody Bar hosts karaoke and other musical ventures. The cover varies but is usually $10 or less.

★ Drake Hotel   BAR

(☑ 416-531-5042; www.thedrakehotel.ca; 1150 Queen St W; ⊙ 11am-2am Mon-Fri, 10am-2am Sat & Sun; ⓰ 501) The Drake is part boutique hotel (d/ste from $312/455; Ⓟ ⊝ ✱ ⓦ), part pub, part live-music venue and part nightclub. There's a bunch of different areas to enjoy, including the chic Sky Yard rooftop bar and the Drake Underground basement.

★ Rooftop   ROOFTOP BAR

(☑ 416-362-8439; www.thebroadviewhotel.ca; Broadview Hotel, 106 Broadview Ave; ⊙ 5pm-late Mon-Thu, 11:30am-late Fri-Sun; ⓰ 501, 502, 503) This rooftop bar, boasting floor-to-ceiling

TORONTO FOR CHILDREN

Toronto is a kid-friendly city with a wide range of options for children of all ages: museums and parks, sights and thrills. The TTC makes it easy – kids travel for free – and most places offer discounted admission rates.

Royal Ontario Museum (p60) Towering dinosaur skeletons, mummies, suits of armor, bat caves, hands-on exhibits and more – much more – keep kiddos engaged at this remarkable museum. Trained facilitators answer questions and provide suggestions on what to do next.

LEGOLAND Discovery Centre (✓1-855-356-2150; www.legolanddiscoverycentre.ca/toronto; 1 Bass Pro Mills Dr, Vaughan; $28; ⊙10am-9pm Mon-Sat, 11am-7pm Sun; P ♿; S Yorkdale) Younger kids with a penchant for Lego will be fascinated by the many building possibilities here. Master builders are on hand to help with projects big and small.

Ontario Science Centre (✓416-696-1000; www.ontariosciencecentre.ca; 770 Don Mills Rd; science center adult/child $22/13, IMAX $13/9, combined ticket $28/19; ⊙10am-5pm Sun-Fri, to 8pm Sat; P ♿; ☐34, 25) Though this center is a bit dated, the hands-on science exhibits, live demonstrations and IMAX theater are hits with children, especially those with lots of questions about how the world around them works.

CN Tower (p57) Teens can experience the ultimate thrill: the EdgeWalk, a 116-story-high walk around the outer perimeter, with nothing between them and the city below. (A tether to a metal rail keeps them safe!)

Canada's Wonderland (✓905-832-8131; www.canadaswonderland.com; 9580 Jane St, Vaughan; day passes $66; ⊙10am-10pm Jun-Aug, Sat & Sun only with earlier closing May & Sep; P; S Vaughan) More than 60 rides, ranging from white-knuckle roller coasters to carousels, keep children of all ages happy at this amusement park. A water park seals the deal.

Centreville Amusement Park (✓416-203-0405; www.centreisland.ca; Centre Island; all-day ride passes adult/child/family $36/27/118; ⊙10:30am-8pm Jun-Aug, Sat & Sun only with earlier closing May & Sep; ♿; ⛴Centre Island) An antique carousel, rides and a miniature train are a thrill for little ones here. A petting zoo is a great backup if the rides prove too scary!

windows and a wraparound patio, affords guests a 360-degree view of Toronto and a breathtaking outlook on the city skyline. Shareables and finger foods – duck-fat popcorn with sea salt, anyone? – complement the cocktail and wine lists well. Sunsets are particularly busy. Reservations are highly recommended.

☆ Entertainment

As you might have guessed, there's always something going on here, from jazz to arthouse cinema, offbeat theater, opera, punk rock and hockey. In summer, free festivals and outdoor concerts are the norm, but Toronto's dance and live-music scene keeps grooving year-round. LGBTIQ+ life is also rich and open, with plenty of clubs, groups, bar nights and activities for all.

Many Torontonians weep with joy at the very mention of their beloved sporting teams: the Blue Jays (✓416-341-1234; www.bluejays.com; 1 Blue Jays Way; ⊙Apr-Sep; ☐510A, 510B) for professional baseball and the Argonauts (✓416-341-2746; www.argonauts. ca; ⊙Jun-Oct; ☐509, 511) for football through the summer; and the Maple Leafs (✓416-815-5982; www.mapleleafs.com; 40 Bay St; ⊙Oct-Apr; S Union) for hockey and the Raptors (✓416-815-5500; www.nba.com/raptors; 40 Bay St; ⊙Oct-Apr; S Union) for basketball. Ticketmaster (www.ticketmaster.ca) sells advance tickets, as do the box offices at Scotiabank Arena (✓416-815-5500; www.scotiabankarena. com; 40 Bay St; S Union) and the Rogers Centre (✓416-341-2770; 1 Blue Jays Way; 1hr tours adult/child $17/10; S Union). Ticket scalping is illegal, but that doesn't seem to stop anybody.

★**Reservoir Lounge** JAZZ
(✓416-955-0887; www.reservoirlounge.com; 52 Wellington St E; cover $5-10; ⊙7:30pm-2am Tue-Sat; ☐503, 504) Swing dancers, jazz singers and blues crooners call this cool, candlelit basement lounge home, and it's hosted its fair share of musical greats over the years.

Where else can you enjoy a martini while dipping strawberries into chocolate fondue during the show? Tables are reserved for diners; prepare to drop at least $15 per person to sit down.

⭐ Horseshoe Tavern
LIVE MUSIC

(☑ 416-598-4226; www.horseshoetavern.com; 370 Queen St W; ⏰ noon-2:30am; 🚇 501, 510) Well past its 70th birthday, the legendary Horseshoe still plays a crucial role in the development of local indie rock. This place oozes a history of good times and classic performances. Come for a beer and check it out.

In terms of not-so-local acts, it was here that The Police played on their first North American tour – Sting did an encore in his underwear – and Bran Van 3000 made their long-awaited comeback.

⭐ Soulpepper
THEATER

(☑ 416-866-8666; www.soulpepper.ca; 50 Tank House Lane; 🚌 72, 🚇 503, 504) This theater company has a repertoire ranging from new works to classics, most focused on the diversity of Canada's voices and identities. Youth-outreach initiatives and theater training programs are shining stars. Housed in the Young Centre for the Performing Arts (www.youngcentre.ca;) in the heart of the Distillery District.

⭐ TIFF Bell Lightbox
CINEMA

(☑ 888-599-8433; www.tiff.net; 350 King St W; 🚇 504) Headquarters of the Toronto International Film Festival (p63), this resplendent cinema complex is the hub of all the action when the festival's in town. Throughout the year it's used primarily for TIFF Cinematheque, screening world cinema, independent films, directorial retrospectives and other special events. Try to see a film here if you can.

🛍 Shopping

Shopping in Toronto is a big deal. When it's -20°C outside, you have to fill the gap between brunch and the movies with *something*, right? People like to update their wardrobes and redecorate their homes, or just walk around the sprawling Eaton Centre (☑ 416-598-8560; www.torontoeatoncentre. com; 220 Yonge St; ⏰ 10am-9:30pm Mon-Fri, 9:30am-9:30pm Sat, 10am-7pm Sun; 📶; 🚇 Queen, Dundas).

This habit continues through to summer, making boutique-hopping an excuse to hit the streets, or vice versa.

⭐ Arts Market
ART

(☑ 416-778-9533; www.artsmarket.ca; 790 Queen St E; ⏰ noon-5pm Mon-Tue, to 6pm Wed-Fri, 11am-6pm Sun; 🚇 501, 502, 503) A collective of local artists displays and sells work at this eclectic shop. High quality and unique, there's everything from handcrafted cards and jewelry to pottery and portraits. A few vintage finds, too.

⭐ Sonic Boom
MUSIC

(☑ 416-532-0334; https://sonicboommusic.com; 215 Spadina Ave; ⏰ 10am-10pm; 🚇 310, 510) The largest indie record store in Canada, Sonic Boom has rows upon rows of new and used vinyl, CDs and even cassettes. Longtime staffers are deeply knowledgeable, offering direction and advice. Quirky T-shirts, irreverent souvenirs and coffee-table books (most with a musical bent) are sold at the front.

⭐ Courage My Love
VINTAGE

(☑ 416-979-1992; 14 Kensington Ave; ⏰ 11am-6pm Mon-Sat, 1-5pm Sun; 🚇 505, 510) Vintage-clothing stores have been around Kensington Market for decades, but Courage My Love amazes fashion mavens with its secondhand slip dresses, retro pants and white dress shirts in a cornucopia of styles. The beads, leather goods and silver jewelry are handpicked. Well stocked without being overwhelming.

⭐ Sunday Antique Market
MARKET

(☑ 416-410-1310; www.facebook.com/SundayAntique Market; St Lawrence Market Complex, 125 The Esplanade; ⏰ 7am-4pm Sun; 🚇 503, 504) Located in a tent-style building at the southern end of the St Lawrence Market Complex (p57), this weekly antique market brings more than 90 vendors to the neighborhood selling everything from delicate tea cups and crystal lamps to phonographs and creepy porcelain dolls. A great place to find a hidden treasure! (One person's trash...) The market should have moved to a new North Market building by the time you read this.

⭐ Glad Day
BOOKS

(☑ 416-901-6600; www.gladdaybookshop.com; 499 Church St; ⏰ 10am-10pm Mon-Thu, to 2am Fri & Sat, 11am-7pm Sun; 🚇 Wellesley) It's the oldest still-running gay bookstore in the world, making Glad Day an LGBTIQ+ landmark. The store has transformed from a place to defy censorship of LGBTIQ+ publications into an event and gathering space to promote creativity and further free speech. It's also a cafe and bar. Weekends mean Saturday-night dance parties and Sunday Drag Brunch.

ℹ️ Information

Ontario Travel Information Centre (☑ 416-314-5899; www.ontariotravel.net; Union Station, 65 Front St W; ⊙ 9am-6pm Mon-Sat, 10am-6pm Sun; ⑤ Union) Knowledgeable multilingual staff and overflowing racks of brochures that cover every nook and cranny of Toronto and beyond.

ℹ️ Getting There & Away

Toronto is wrapped in a mesh of multilane highways that are frequently crippled by congestion. The Gardiner Expwy runs west along the lakeshore into Queen Elizabeth Way (QEW) to Niagara Falls. At the city's western border, Hwy 427 runs north to the airport. Hwy 401 is the main east–west arterial and is regularly jammed. On the eastern side of the city, the Don Valley Pkwy connects Hwy 401 to the Gardiner Expwy. Hwys 400 and 404 run north from Toronto. A GPS is strongly recommended.

NIAGARA PENINSULA

Jutting east from Hamilton and forming a natural divide between Lake Erie and Lake Ontario, the Niagara Peninsula is a legitimate tourist hot spot. Though many see only the falls and Clifton Hill on a day tour from Toronto, there's lots to explore here. Consider a several-day visit to fully experience the delights of the peninsula.

Water flows from Lake Erie, 100m higher than Lake Ontario, via two avenues: stepping down steadily through the locks along the Welland Canal, or surging over Niagara Falls in a reckless, swollen torrent. A steep limestone escarpment jags along the spine of the peninsula, generating a unique microclimate. Humid and often frost free, this is prime terrain for viticulture, a fact not lost on the award-winning wineries of Niagara-on-the-Lake.

Niagara Falls

☑ 905 / POP 88,100

An unstoppable flow of rushing water surges over the arcing fault in the riverbed with thunderous force. Great plumes of icy mist rise for hundreds of meters as the waters collide, like an ethereal veil concealing the vast rift behind the torrent. Thousands of onlookers delight in the spectacle every day, drawn by the force of the current and the hypnotic mist.

Otherwise, Niagara might not be what you expect: the town feels like a tacky, out-dated amusement park. It has been a saucy honeymoon destination ever since Napoleon's brother brought his bride here – tags like 'For newlyweds and nearly deads' and 'Viagra Falls' are apt. A crass morass of casinos, sleazy motels and tourist traps lines Clifton Hill and Lundy's Lane – a Little Las Vegas! Love it or loathe it, there's nowhere quite like it.

☉ Sights

Parking access for sights and activities around the falls and Clifton Hill is expensive and limited.

☉ The Falls & Around

Niagara Falls forms a natural rift between Ontario and New York State. On the US side, Bridal Veil Falls and the adjacent American Falls crash onto mammoth fallen rocks. On the Canadian side, the grander, more powerful Horseshoe Falls FREE plunge into the cloudy Maid of the Mist Pool. The prime falls-watching spot is Table Rock FREE, poised just meters from the drop. At sunset, the falls also are illuminated, in changing colors, year-round – a whimsical and beautiful sight.

Niagara is not the tallest of the world's waterfalls (it ranks a lowly 50th) but in terms of sheer volume, there's nothing like it – more than 8500 bathtubs of water plummet downward every second. By day or night, regardless of the season, the falls never fail to awe: 12 million visitors annually can't be wrong. Even in winter, when the flow is partially hidden and the edges freeze solid, the watery extravaganza is undiminished. Very occasionally the falls stop altogether. This happened on Easter Sunday morning in 1848, when ice completely jammed the flow.

Tickets for the four falls attractions listed below can be purchased separately, but the online 27% discounted Niagara Falls Adventure Classic Pass (www.niagaraparks.com; adult/child $65/43) is better value. It includes a ride on Hornblower Niagara Cruises (p71) and admission to the Journey Behind the Falls (p71), White Water Walk (☑ 877-642-7275; 4330 Niagara Pkwy; adult/child $14/9; ⊙ 9am-9pm Apr-Oct) and Niagara's Fury (☑ 905-358-3268; www.niagaraparks.com; 6650 Niagara Pkwy; adult/child $16/10.25; ⊙ half-hourly 9:15am-9pm; ♿), plus two days' transportation on the WEGO bus system. If you want to go all out, upgrade to the Niagara Falls Adventure Pass Plus (adult/child $90/59), which includes everything on the Classic Pass plus admission to the Floral Showhouse (☑905-354-1721; www.niagaraparks.com; 7145 Niagara Pkwy; adult/child $7/4; ☺9:30am-5pm; ℗), Butterfly Conservatory (p21), nearby historic sites, WEGO service to Niagara-on-the-Lake and unlimited rides on the Incline Railway (☑877-642-7275; www.niagaraparks.com; 6635 Niagara Pkwy; one way $2.50, day passes $6.25). Passes are also available from the Niagara Parks Commission at Table Rock Information Centre (p73), the Ontario Travel Information (p73) center and most attractions.

◉ Clifton Hill

Clifton Hill is a street name, but refers to a broader area near the falls occupied by a sensory bombardment of artificial enticements. House of Frankenstein, Louis Tussaud's Waxworks, Castle Dracula – they're all here. In most cases, paying the admission will leave you feeling kinda like a sucker.

★Skylon Tower   VIEWPOINT
(☑905-356-2651; www.skylon.com; 5200 Robinson St; adult/child $16.25/10.50; ☺9am-10pm Mon-Thu, to 11pm Fri-Sun; ℗) The Skylon Tower is a 158m concrete spire with yellow pill-shaped elevators crawling up and down the tower's neck to the top. The interior itself is dated, even a little sad, but the views! They're eye-popping and simply picture perfect, with the falls to the east and, on clear days, Toronto to the north. The two observation areas – a glass-enclosed indoor deck and a wire-fenced outdoor one – give you 360-degree views of the region. Plus, there's a revolving restaurant and a family-friendly buffet.

🎿 Activities & Tours

★Hornblower Niagara Cruises   BOATING
(www.niagaracruises.com; 5920 Niagara Pkwy; adult/child $26/16, fireworks cruise $40; ☺8:30am-8:30pm May-Sep, to 5:30pm Oct) A classic Niagara Falls experience: boat tours that come so close to the spectacular Bridal Veil Falls and Horseshoe Falls that you'll be drenched (despite the rain ponchos). Hornblower offers two tours on its 700-person catamarans: a 20-minute daytime 'Voyage to the Falls'; and a 40-minute 'Fireworks Cruise,' under the fireworks on summer nights with live music and cash bar. Avoid the massive ticket lines and buy a ticket online.

★Journey Behind the Falls   WALKING
(☑905-354-1551; www.niagaraparks.com; 6650 Niagara Pkwy; adult/child $22/14; ☺9am-10pm, hours vary by season) From Table Rock Information Centre, don a very unsexy plastic poncho and take an elevator through the bedrock partway down the cliff to the Cataract and Great Falls portals for an in-your-face view of the falls. Continue through 130-year-old-tunnels to two observation decks – as close as you can get to the falls without hopping in a barrel. It's open year-round, but be prepared to queue. In winter the lower deck is usually closed.

Niagara River Recreation Trail   WALKING
(www.niagaraparks.com) The idyllic 3m-wide Niagara River Recreation Trail, for cycling, jogging and walking, runs parallel to the slow-roaming, leafy Niagara Pkwy. The trail can easily be divided into four chunks, each of which takes around two hours to pedal. The parkway meanders for 56km along the Niagara River, from Niagara-on-the-Lake past the falls and all the way to Fort Erie.

Niagara Helicopters   SCENIC FLIGHTS
(☑905-357-5672; www.niagarahelicopters.com; 3731 Victoria Ave; adult/child $149/92; ☺9am-sunset, weather permitting) A fantastic 12-minute falls encounter takes you on a flight path along the Niagara River, over the Whirlpool past the American Falls (p70) and Bridal Veil Falls (p70) for the grand finale over Horseshoe Falls (p70). Learn facts about the sights via clunky headphones. A gorgeous and pricey (and not the most environmentally sensitive) way to see the falls.

🎊 Festivals & Events

Summer Fireworks Series   FIREWORKS
(www.niagarafallstourism.com; ☺May-Oct) A magnificent fireworks show takes place over the falls during the summer months: huge, sparkling lights and multicolored puffs light up the skies and the roaring falls below. The show starts at 10pm and is held nightly from June to August and on weekends in May, September and October. For a great view, stake out a spot near Table Rock (p70), see it from the water on a Hornblower (p71) boat tour, or head to the top of the Skylon (p71).

Winter Festival of Lights   LIGHT SHOW
(☑905-374-1616; www.wfol.com; ☺mid-Nov–mid-Jan; 🚌) FREE A season of events from mid-November to mid-January including concerts, fireworks, more than 125 animated

displays and two million tree- and ground lights. The undisputed highlight, though, is an over-the-top nocturnal light display along an 8km route, which is lit daily from 5pm to midnight.

🛏 Sleeping

There are usually more beds than heads in Niagara Falls, but the town is sometimes completely booked up. Prices spike sharply in summer, on weekends and during holidays. Cheap motels line Lundy's Lane. If you are coming from Toronto just for the falls, it really isn't necessary to stay overnight; a day trip is plenty.

Hostelling International
Niagara Falls   HOSTEL $
(☑ 905-357-0770; www.hostellingniagara.com; 4549 Cataract Ave; dm/d incl breakfast from $39/98; P @ 🛜) Quietly adrift in the old town, this homey, multicolored hostel sleeps around 90 people. The facilities, including a sizable and well-stocked kitchen, pool table, lockers and cool basement lounge, are in good shape; staff are friendly and eco-focused. It's close to the train and bus stations, and bikes are available for rent. Rates drop a bit in the winter.

★ Cadillac Motel   MOTEL $$
(☑ 905-356-0830; www.cadillacmotelniagara.com; 5342 Ferry St; r $199; P ✳ 🛜) A retro motel just west of the kitsch on Clifton Hill, rooms here are modern and chic with great beds and luxe linens. Each has a classic Caddy theme – mostly, a photo mural of vintage Cadillacs or models like the pink Fleetwood convertible made famous by Elvis. Outside, Adirondack chairs add to the throw-back feel. Reservations recommended in the summer.

★ Marriott Niagara Falls   HOTEL $$
(☑ 888-501-8916; www.niagarafallsmarriott.com; 6740 Fallsview Blvd; r from $224; P ⇄ ✳ @ 🛜 🛀) This sprawling giant is so close that you could almost touch the falls...the lobby itself seems to hang over the Horseshoe Falls (p70). A variety of modern room types is available, but many love the two-level loft suites with hot tub, fireplace and spectacular views from the floor-to-ceiling windows. To save some cash, opt for a city-view room.

Park Place Bed
& Breakfast   B&B $$
(☑ 905-358-0279; www.parkplaceniagara.ca; 4851 River Rd; r from $150; P ⇄ ✳ 🛜) A gorgeous Queen Anne Revival–style house with a wrap-around verandah and lush gardens is the setting for this B&B. There are just two rooms and a carriage house, each unique in style and layout – one has a jacuzzi, another a working fireplace – but equally upscale. A full breakfast, prepared to order, is offered each morning. The affable owners are a font of regional information.

🍴 Eating

The old downtown section of town has seen many failed revival attempts, but it's worth checking out for new restaurants, if the other options aren't appealing. Fast food (and dressed-up, overpriced fast food) is abundant in the touristy strip, but the best eats can be found a little further afield. For cuisine a cut above, head up the road to Niagara-on-the-Lake.

Queen Charlotte Tea Room   BRITISH $
(☑ 905-371-1350; www.thequeencharlottetearoom. com; 5689 Main St; mains $8-17, high tea $25; ⊙ 11am-7pm Wed, Thu, Sat & Sun, to 8pm Fri) British expats craving a decent or even fancy cuppa, cucumber sandwiches, steak and kidney or fish-and-chips with mushy peas should head straight to this quaint establishment on Main St, near the intersection with Lundy's Lane, for a spot of tiffin! Reservations required for high tea; gluten-free options too.

Paris Crepes Cafe   FRENCH $$
(☑ 289-296-4218; www.pariscrepescafe.ca; 4613 Queen St; mains $17-33; ⊙ 11am-2pm & 5-8pm Mon-Fri, 10am-2pm & 5-8:30pm Sat & Sun) In the revitalized area of Queen St you'll find this quaint creperie, a very long way from the streets of Paris: you can't miss the dark-red building. Sweet and savory crepe sensations are served among other continental delights from the wonderfully authentic Parisian menu.

Napoli Ristorante Pizzeria   ITALIAN $$
(☑ 905-356-3345; www.napoliristorante.ca; 5545 Ferry St; mains $16-36; ⊙ 4:30-10pm) Head to Napoli for the best Italian in town, hands down. Delicious pizza, rich pasta, creamy risotto and veal parmigiana all feature on the menu.

Koutouki Greek Cuisine   GREEK $$$
(☑ 905-354-6776; http://koutoukiniagara.com; 5745 Ferry St; mains $22-42; ⊙ 4-10pm Tue-Sun) A local favorite with an old-world feel, Koutouki serves classic Greek cuisine with a homey but elegant touch. Meals are beautifully presented and filling. Try, if you can, to save room for the baklava, a sweet phyllo dough dessert with walnuts and honey syrup. Worth the longish walk from the falls.

DAREDEVILS

Surprisingly, more than a few people who have gone over Niagara Falls have actually lived to tell the tale. The first successful leap was in 1901, by a 63-year-old schoolteacher named Annie Taylor, who did it in a skirt, no less. This prompted a rash of barrel stunters that continued into the 1920s, including Bobby Leach, who survived the drop but met his untimely death after slipping on an orange peel and developing gangrene!

In 1984 Karl Soucek revived the tradition in a bright-red barrel. He made it, only to die six months later in another barrel stunt in Houston. Also during the 1980s, two locals successfully took the plunge lying head to head in the same barrel.

A US citizen who tried to jet ski over the falls in 1995 might have made it – if his rocket-propelled parachute had opened. Another American, Kirk Jones, survived the trip over the falls unaided in 2003. After being charged by Canadian police with illegally performing a stunt, he joined the circus.

Only one accidental falls-faller has survived – a seven-year-old Tennessee boy who fell out of a boat upstream in 1960 and survived the drop without even breaking a bone.

Take the virtual plunge at the Niagara IMAX (☑ 905-358-3611; www.imaxniagara.com; 6170 Fallsview Blvd; adult/child IMAX $13/9.50, Daredevil Exhibit $8/6.50, combo $15.50/13; ☉ 9am-9pm; ℗ 🎦), and check out the over-the-falls barrels folks have used at the Daredevil Exhibit.

AG CANADIAN **$$$**
(☑ 289-292-0005; www.agcuisine.com; 5195 Magdalen St; mains $18-38; ☉ 6-9:30pm Tue-Sun) Fine dining isn't something you find easily at the falls, which makes this fine restaurant at the Sterling Inn & Spa (☑ 289-292-0000; www.sterlingniagara.com; r from $221; 🛜) so refreshing. Service, decor, presentation and especially the quality of the food all rate highly. It has a seasonal menu featuring dishes like fennel-pollen pickerel, coffee-roasted venison and crispy-skinned trout.

☆ Entertainment

Music in the Park LIVE MUSIC
(Queen Victoria Park, 6345 Niagara Pkwy; ☉ 8-10pm Thu-Sun Jun-Sep) FREE On summer weekend nights, check out local talent during free classic-rock concerts at Queen Victoria Park, facing the American Falls (p70). The music starts at 8pm and ends as the fireworks (p71) begin. A great way to spend a warm evening by the falls.

❶ Information

Niagara Falls Tourism (☑ 905-356-6061; www.niagarafallstourism.com; 6815 Stanley Ave; ☉ 9am-5pm Mon-Fri) Offers information on the different neighborhoods and what's on around town. Located near the Marriott (p72).

Niagara Parks Welcome Centre (Table Rock Visitor Centre; ☑ 877-642-7275; www.niagaraparks.com; 6650 Niagara Pkwy; ☉ 9am-9pm, to 7pm Sep-May) Niagara Parks Commission has five welcome centers in the most touristed sections of the falls, where visitors can gather information and purchase tickets to area sights. The one at **Table Rock Visitor Centre**, in front of Horseshoe Falls (p70), is especially convenient. Other locations include near the Hornblower Niagara Cruises (p71) ticket booth and in Clifton Hill. Check the website for more details.

Ontario Travel Information (☑ 905-358-3221; www.ontariotravel.net; 5355 Stanley Ave; ☉ 8:30am-5:30pm Sun-Thu, to 6pm Fri & Sat Jun-Aug, 8:30am-4:30pm Sep-May) On the western outskirts of town; offers free tourist booklets containing maps and discount coupons. Discounted tickets to area sights, including Niagara Falls Adventure Passes, are sold here too.

❶ Getting Around

Driving and parking around the center is an expensive headache, sometimes costing up to $30 per day. Park at the Niagara IMAX lot for just $10 for the whole day and walk, or follow the parking district signs and stash the car for the day (around $6 per 30 minutes, or $15 per day). In the winter, the Falls Casino occasionally offers spots for $5 per day. The huge Rapidsview parking lot (also the WEGO depot) is 3km south of the falls off River Rd. See the website for all the locations: www.niagarafallstourism.com/plan/parking.

Put on your sneakers and get t'steppin' – walking is the way to go! You'll only need wheels to visit outlying sights along the Niagara Pkwy or if you're staying on Lundy's Lane. There is very little shade along the falls vantage points; in the summer be sure to wear a hat.

JOANNE DALE/SHUTTERSTOCK. DESIGNER TOM RIDOUT ©

Voices of Freedom Memorial

Niagara-on-the-Lake

📞 905 / POP 17,500

One of the best-preserved 19th-century towns in North America, affluent N-o-t-L is an undeniably gorgeous place, with tree-lined streets, lush parks and impeccably restored houses. Originally a Neutral First Nations village, the current town was founded by Loyalists from New York State after the American Revolution, later becoming the first capital of the colony of Upper Canada. Today, lovely Queen St teems with shops of the 'ye olde' variety selling antiques, Brit-style souvenirs and homemade fudge. Tour-bus visitors take over the streets, puffing Cuban cigars and dampening the charm; the town fountain is full of coins but there are no homeless people here to plunder it. Is this a *real* town, or just gingerbread? Is there a soul beneath the surface? Yes, after 5pm.

👁 Sights & Tours

Voices of Freedom Memorial MEMORIAL
(www.vofpark.org; 244 Regent St) Celebrating and honoring the contributions of Black Canadians to Niagara-on-the-Lake, this experiential art installation integrates West African and Underground Railroad symbolism with historical city footprints of Black neighborhoods and inspirational quotes. A beautifully manicured garden surrounds it. Download the walking tour app from the website. A place to reflect and meditate.

Fort George HISTORIC SITE
(📞 905-468-6614; www.pc.gc.ca/fortgeorge; 51 Queens Pde; adult/child $11.70/free; ⊙ 10am-5pm May-Oct, noon-4pm Sat & Sun only Nov-Apr; P 🐾) On the town's southeastern fringe, restored Fort George dates from 1797. The fort saw some bloody battles during the War of 1812, changing hands between British and US forces a couple of times. Within the spiked battlements are officers' quarters, a working kitchen, a powder magazine and storage houses.

Ghost tours, skills demonstrations, retro tank displays and battle reenactments occur throughout the summer. Knowledgeable staff dressed in military garb and period dress serve as interpreters and give talks. Parking costs $6.

Niagara Historical Society Museum MUSEUM
(📞 905-468-3912; www.niagarahistorical.museum; 43 Castlereagh St; adult/child $5/1; ⊙ 10am-5pm May-Oct, from 1pm Nov-Apr; P) A vast collection relating to the town's past, ranging from First Nations artifacts to Loyalist and War of 1812 collectibles (including the prized hat of Major-General Sir Isaac Brock). There also is an exhibit chronicling the changing demographics of Niagara-on-the-Lake, from the pre-colonial Neutral Nation to modern-day winemakers. Self-guided tours, including a guide to Black Canadian history, are available in several languages. It's south of Simcoe Park.

Whirlpool Jet Boat Tours
BOATING

(📞 905-468-4800; www.whirlpooljet.com; 61 Melville St; adult/child $94/61; ☺Apr-Oct; 🅿) A wet and wild ride, full of fishtails and splashy stops on 1500-horsepower jet boats. The ride lasts about an hour, heading upriver toward the falls, through Class V rapids, and turning around right before the Whirlpool. Bring a change of clothes (and maybe underwear); water shoes are recommended. Reservations required.

🛏 Sleeping & Eating

Although there are more than 100 small inns and B&Bs in town, accommodations are expensive and often booked out. Plan ahead.

Charles Hotel
HOTEL $$$

(📞 800-474-0632; www.niagarasfinest.com/charles; 209 Queen St; d from $295; 🅿 ❄ ❇ 🛜) This lovable, romantic little hotel (c 1832) has a sweeping verandah overlooking the golf course and Lake Ontario. Rooms of varying sizes are sumptuously decorated in a diverse range of styles. Each is wonderfully comfortable – there's even a pillow menu.

Prince of Wales Hotel
HOTEL $$$

(📞 905-468-3246; www.vintage-hotels.com; 6 Picton St; d/ste from $370/510; 🅿 ❄ ❇ 🛜 🏊) Prince of N-o-t-L, an elegant Victorian hotel, was knocked into shape around 1864 and retains much of its period primp: vaulted ceilings, timber-inlay floors and red-waistcoated bellhops. Frills and floral prints seem angled toward the elderly and honeymooners, but it's the perfect spot for anyone looking to splash out in a colonial British sort of way.

Also on-site are a spa, afternoon tea and its elegant restaurant, Noble. A resort fee of $15 is tacked onto the daily bill.

⭐ Pieza Pizzeria
PIZZA $$

(📞 289-868-9191; www.piezapizzeria.com; 188 Victoria St; pizzas $17-22; ☺noon-9pm Tue-Sun; 🍴🅿) A cute turn-of-the-century house repurposed into an even cuter pizzeria with simple, streamlined decor. It's the pizza that speaks loudest here: dough made from imported Italian flour, hand-crushed tomatoes, fresh mozzarella, gourmet toppings and a *pizzaiuolo* (pizza maker) born and raised in Naples. An impressive 2200kg wood-burning oven sits in the open kitchen.

Noble
FUSION $$$

(📞 905-468-3246; www.vintage-hotels.com/princeof wales/noble.php; 6 Picton St; mains $16-52; ☺7-11am, noon-2:30pm & 5:30-9pm) The fine-dining room at the opulent Prince of Wales Hotel takes its food seriously. The contemporary menu offers taste inventions like a tart of locally cured prosciutto, cacciatore sausage, tomato and mascarpone, followed by grilled venison with hominy and sweet corn succotash, pine mushrooms and Bordelaise sauce. Leave room for dessert (you've been warned). Tasting menu available.

ℹ Information

Chamber of Commerce Visitors Information Centre (📞 905-468-1950; www.niagaraonthelake.com; 26 Queen St; ☺10am-6pm) A brochure-filled info center in the basement of the old courthouse. Pick up the *Niagara-on-the-Lake Official Visitors' Guide* for maps and a self-guided walking tour.

NORTHERN ONTARIO

'Big' is a theme in Northern Ontario. The area is so vast that it could fit six Englands and still have room for a Scotland or two. Industry is big here, too: most of the world's silver and nickel ore comes from local mines, while boundless forests have made the region a key timber producer. What's not so big is the local population; as of the most recent census, none of the cities has over 100,000 residents. Two main highways weave an intersecting course across the province. Hwy 17 (the Trans-Canada) unveils the area's scenic pièce de résistance, the northern crest over Lake Superior. From Sudbury, misty fjordlike passages hide isolated beaches among dense thickets of pine, cedar and birch.

Killarney Provincial Park

The 645-sq-km Killarney Provincial Park covers vast expanses of Georgian Bay shoreline and is home to moose, black bears, beavers and deer, as well as over 100 bird species. The Group of Seven artists had a cabin near Hwy 6 (just west of the park) and were instrumental in its 1964 establishment; today the park is considered to be one of the finest kayaking destinations in the world. Killarney's 80km La Cloche Silhouette Trail is a rugged trek for experienced hikers that twists through a mountainous realm of sapphire lakes, thirsty birches, luscious pine forests and shimmering quartzite cliffs. A network of shorter, less challenging hikes also offers glimpses of the majestic terrain, including the Cranberry Bog Trail (a 4km loop) and the Granite Ridge Trail (a 2km loop). Killarney Kanoes (p29) provides canoe and kayak rentals, while Killarney Outfitters (☑888-222-3410, 705-287-2828; www.killarneyoutfitters.com; 1076 Hwy 637, Killarney; canoe & kayak rental per day $42-64) offers equipment rentals and fully outfitted packages (just bring your toothbrush!) for hiking, canoeing, kayaking and stand-up paddleboarding.

🛏 Sleeping

Killarney Mountain Lodge LODGE $$
(☑705-287-2242, 800-461-1117; www.killarney.com; 3 Commissioner St, Killarney; d/ste incl breakfast from $200/269; ☺May-Oct; �🔹🟢) In Killarney village, this wooden compound with waterfront accommodations is run by canoeing, kayaking and hiking buffs Killarney Outfitters. The beautiful pine rooms, cabins, suites and chalets all provide a luxurious experience of the wilderness, with views of George Island across the Killarney Channel. There's a restaurant and a sauna for unwinding after a long day in the park.

🛍 Shopping

Grundy Lake Supply Post SPORTS & OUTDOORS
(☑705-383-2251; www.grundylakesupplypost.com; 20395 Hwy 522 East; ☺9am-5pm mid-May–early Jul, 8am-9pm early Jul-early Oct) Now located 1km off Hwy 69 down Hwy 522, the renovated Grundy Lake Supply Post has everything one would need for a camping adventure, including boat and canoe rentals, as well as gas and a small on-site cafe. If coming from the south, this is the closest shop to stock up on supplies before going into Killarney Provincial Park.

Sudbury
☑705 / POP 88,054
Sudbury gets props for making something out of nothing. In the 1880s it was but a desolate lumber camp called Ste-Anne-des-Pins. Then, when the Canadian Pacific Railway plowed through in 1883, the discovery of a mother lode of nickel-copper ore transformed the dreary region into the biggest nickel producer worldwide. By 1920 industrial toxicity and acid rain had killed the trees and fouled the soil, leaving Sudbury a bleak place of blackened boulders. So barren was the surrounding terrain that NASA came here to train in the 1960s. Today the story is more environmentally friendly:

as part of the city's 'regreening' program, locals have planted over 9.1 million trees since 1978, although heavy industry and mining still rule. Sudbury has a university, two fantastic science museums, some cool haunts and chilled locals, but there's little reason to visit unless you're passing through, particularly in winter when a lot of tourist businesses close.

◎ Sights

★**Science North** MUSEUM
(☑705-522-3701; www.sciencenorth.ca; 100 Ramsey Lake Rd; adult/child from $27/23; ☺10am-4pm, to 5pm Sat & Sun May-Aug) After passing through a tunnel dug deep within the 2.5-billion-year-old Canadian Shield, work your way down through the spiral of exciting hands-on activities in this fantastic museum. Wander through a living butterfly garden, stargaze in the digital planetarium (adult/child $8/6) or fly away on a bush-plane simulator. Visiting exhibits and IMAX films change regularly.

Dynamic Earth MUSEUM
(☑705-522-3701; www.dynamicearth.ca; 122 Big Nickel Rd; adult/child $22/18, parking $6 in summer; ☺9am-6pm Apr-Oct) Dynamic Earth's main attraction is the underground tour with simulated dynamite blast. Visitors stand to learn lots about geology and our planet from thought-provoking interactive exhibits. In summer, tours leave roughly every 30 minutes from 10am to 3:30pm.

🛏 Sleeping & Eating

Radisson Sudbury BUSINESS HOTEL $$
(☑705-675-1123; www.radissonsudbury.com; 85 St Anne Rd; d from $116; 🅿🔹🟢) The Radisson offers 147 comfortable rooms in a central location. Service and finish are a cut above its competitors, and facilities include a pool, hot tub, fitness center and guest laundry. Guests can wander into the adjoining Rainbow Centre mall for a food court and grocery store. The resident Italian restaurant, Pesto's, also serves breakfast, lunch and dinner.

Holiday Inn BUSINESS HOTEL $$
(☑705-522-3000; www.holidayinn.com; 1696 Regent St; d from $119; 🅿🔹🟢) From the outside, this Holiday Inn looks frozen in 1972. Inside are refurbished, ~~generic rooms of a good~~ size. There's an indoor pool, hot tub and fitness center. A room with breakfast is an extra $10, or you can eat an à la carte breakfast in the restaurant.

Motley Kitchen CAFE $
(☎705-222-6685; www.themotleykitchen.com; 70 Young St; mains $14; ⊙11am-3pm Tue-Fri, 10am-2pm Sat & Sun) Sudbury's most popular brunch spot serves unlikely dishes such as breakfast burritos, Welsh rarebit, Croatian crepes, and French toast stuffed with bananas and Nutella or strawberries and yogurt. Plates are garnished with home fries and fresh fruit, and weekday lunches of tacos, sandwiches and salads are served. The only drawback is the popularity can mean the food arrives slowly.

★**Respect is Burning** ITALIAN $$
(☎705-675-5777; www.ribsupperclub.com; 82 Durham St; mains $19-35; ⊙5-10pm Mon-Thu, to 1am Fri & Sat; 🛜) This self-proclaimed supper club's focus is on rustic Tuscan cuisine, but chefs aren't shy about getting experimental. The ever-shifting menu promises bursting flavors with every bite. Weekend evenings feature delectable sample platters and late-night drinks. It can get busy so best to make a reservation.

🍷 Drinking & Entertainment

★**Laughing Buddha** BAR
(☎705-673-2112; www.laughingbuddhasudbury.com; 194 Elgin St; ⊙11am-2am Wed-Sat, to 11pm Sun-Tue) Sudbury's prime hangout for hipsters and slackers pulls off snobby sandwiches (such as the 'Brie LT'; $9) and pizzas ($13) while maintaining an uberchill vibe. In summer slip out to the crimson-brick courtyard and enjoy your casual lunch or one of the many types of craft beer.

HardRock42 PUB
(☎705-586-3303; www.hardrock42.com; 117 Elm St; ⊙7am-11pm Mon-Fri, from 8am Sat, 8am-2pm Sun) Don't let its location inside a chain motel put you off, as HardRock42 has the largest selection of taps in Sudbury and a large enough clientele to make sure the beer is fresh. Food portions (mains from $16) are large and the bar is always full of friendly locals keen for a chat.

Towne House Tavern LIVE MUSIC
(☎705-674-6883; www.thetownehouse.com; 206 Elgin St; ⊙11am-2am Mon-Sat, from noon Sun) This beloved grungy venue is all about Canadian indie from punk to gospel, and stages acts including local bands and big names from the south. Adding to the musical entertainment are a games room and a bar serving pub grub with outside seating.

ℹ️ Information

Greater Sudbury Development Corporation
(☎1-866-451-8525; www.sudburytourism.ca; Tom Davies Sq, 200 Brady St; ⊙8:30am-4:30pm Mon-Fri) Help and brochures.

Sault Ste Marie

☑705 / POP 66.313

'The Soo,' as it's commonly known, quietly governs the narrow rapids between Lakes Huron and Superior. Perched alongside the US border and the St Lawrence Seaway, the sleepy city is the unofficial gateway to the far-flung regions of northwestern Ontario. Originally known as Baawitigong ('Place of the Rapids'), it was a traditional gathering place for the Ojibwe and remains a strong First Nations area today. French fur traders changed the name to Sault Ste Marie (*soo-saynt muh-ree*) or 'St Mary's Falls,' but don't expect to see any waterfalls today: they've been tamed into a series of gargantuan locks. Let's face it, Sault Ste Marie is not the prettiest city. Nonetheless, the Soo is a friendly place and a logical overnight stop on Trans-Canada itineraries. There's a US border crossing here too.

⊙ Sights & Tours

Art Gallery of Algoma GALLERY
(☎705-949-9067; www.artgalleryofalgoma.com; 10 East St; adult/student/child under 12yr $7/5/free; ⊙9am-5pm Tue & Thu-Sat, to 7pm Wed, noon-5pm Sun Jun-Oct) Behind the library, this gallery has a permanent collection and seasonal exhibitions to inspire Group of Seven–themed trips along Lake Superior. Especially in summer, paintings by the group of local scenes are exhibited alongside the work of local First Nations artists.

**Canadian Bushplane
Heritage Centre** MUSEUM
(☎705-945-6242; www.bushplane.com; 50 Pim St; adult/child/student $13.50/3/8; ⊙9am-6pm mid-May–early Oct, 10am-4pm mid-Oct–early-May; 🎫) A visit to the Soo's most dynamic and kid-friendly museum is a great way to get a sense of how Northern Ontario works: bush planes are crucial to remote communities that are not accessible by road. Stroll among retired aircraft, housed in a former government hangar dating from 1924, to see how tiny these flyers really are. A flight simulator takes passengers on a spirited ride along sapphire lakes and towering pines.

ONTARIO SAULT STE MARIE

Agawa Canyon Tour Train RAIL

(ACR; ☎855-768-4171, reservations 800-461-6020; www.agawatrain.com; 129 Bay St; adult/child $101/55; ⊙late Jun–mid-Oct) Constructed in 1899 to facilitate the transport of raw materials to Sault Ste Marie's industrial plants, the Algoma Central Railway is a 475km stretch of railroad from Sault Ste Marie due north to Hearst. Nowadays it transports tour guests through unspoiled wilderness along the pristine lakes and jagged granite of the Canadian Shield.

🛏 Sleeping & Eating

The bulk of motels are found along Great Northern Rd, near Hwy 17, lined with fast-food restaurants and malls. There are also several options scattered downtown, mostly on Bay St, where there's some scenic interest in the waterfront and the majority of attractions, but few amenities after dark.

★ Water Tower Inn HOTEL $$

(☎705-949-8111, 888-461-7077; www.watertowerinn.com; 360 Great Northern Rd; d from $139; P❄🖳🛋) Offering a resort for the price of a room, the Water Tower continues to stand out from the rest with its indoor and outdoor pools, grill-house bar-restaurant, pizza-slinging pub and treatment spa. Room types include family rooms and suites. It's just off Hwy 17, 3.5km northeast of downtown; shuttles to town and the airport are available.

Algonquin Hotel HISTORIC HOTEL $$

(☎705-253-2311; 864 Queen St E; d from $75; P🖳) Built in 1888, this historical building is located close to the Soo's restaurant and shopping district. It's one of the cheaper places in town, but rooms still have comfortable, clean beds with TVs. It's worth paying a bit more for an en suite.

★ Arturo's Ristorante ITALIAN $$$

(☎705-253-0002; www.arturoristorante.com; 515 Queen St E; mains $24-45; ⊙5-10pm Tue-Thu, to 10:30pm Fri & Sat) A shimmering jewel in a dismal downtown strip, decades-old Arturo's is the kind of place you remember after your vacation has ended. Atmospheric but unpretentious with soft lighting, starched white tablecloths and European scenes on the walls, its Italian mains such as veal marsala and chicken *piccata* (with lemon and capers) are tender and succulent, the sauces rich, and the wines appropriately paired.

☆ Entertainment

LopLops LIVE MUSIC

(☎705-945-0754; www.loplops.com; 651 Queen St E; ⊙4pm-2am Wed-Sat) Grab a glass of vino or local craft beer from the glittering steel bar and enjoy an evening amid strumming guitars and the restless murmurs of tortured artists. Promoting local culture since 2003, LopLops stages live music year-round.

❶ Information

Algoma Kinniwabi Travel Association
(☎800-263-2546; www.algomacountry.com; 334 Bay St; ⊙8:30am-4:30pm Mon-Fri) Helpful office (and website) providing information and inspiration for travels along Lake Superior and into the hinterland.

Ontario Travel Information Centre (☎705-945-6941; www.ontariotravel.net; 261 Queen St W; ⊙8:30am-4:30pm) Sells permits for camping, fishing and hunting in the surrounding backcountry, and offers seasonal reports on where to catch the best fall colors, spring blossoms and snow. Near the International Bridge, it has a currency exchange.

Tourism Sault Ste Marie (☎800-461-6020; www.saulttourism.com; Level 1, Civic Centre, 99 Foster Dr; ⊙8:30am-4:30pm Mon-Fri) Stocks brochures and guides covering the Soo. In the Economic Development Corporation office.

Lake Superior Shoreline

Its name befitting its size and beauty, Lake Superior covers a surface area of 82,100 sq km: it's the largest freshwater lake on the planet, with its own ecosystem and microclimate. Much of its dazzling Canadian shoreline is hugged by the Trans-Canada Hwy (at this point Hwy 17), with the drive from Wawa to Sault Ste Marie regarded by some as one of the most picturesque on the highway's 8030km span. A 90km stretch of highway passes directly through Lake Superior Provincial Park. The Great Lake freezes over for many months at a time and most businesses and parks here are seasonal (May to October). Keep an eye out for scraggly moose as you drive the highway, especially at dusk and dawn.

Lake Superior Provincial Park PARK

(☎park office 705-856-2284, visitor centre 705-882-2026; www.ontarioparks.com/park/lakesuperior; Hwy 17; day use per vehicle $14.50/5.25/7.50, campsites $41.25-46.90, backcountry camping adult/child

$10.17/5.09; ☺ Agawa Bay Visitors Centre 9am-8pm Jun-Sep, to 5pm late May & early Oct) Lake Superior Provincial Park protects 1600 sq km of misty fjord-like passages, thick evergreen forest and tranquil sandy coves that feel like they've never known the touch of humankind. The best bits of the park require some level of hiking or canoeing to access, but if you're not so inclined or have limited time, there are numerous picture-perfect vistas just off the highway, which goes straight through the park. Sights and facilities generally open from May to October.

Your first stop should be the Agawa Bay Visitors Centre, 9km in from the park's southern boundary. The interactive museum and park experts will advise you well. There's a smaller information area at Red Rock Lake, 53km further north, if you're coming from the other direction. If you plan to stop in the park, you must buy a permit, but you do not need one if you will be driving straight through on Hwy 17.

Katherine Cove and Old Woman Bay picnic areas, both by the road, have panoramas of misty sand-strewn shores. Budding anthropologists will appreciate the Agawa Rock Pictographs: between 150 and 400 years old, the red-ocher images comprise a spiritual site for the Ojibwe, one of Canada's largest First Nations groups. A rugged 500m trail leads from near the visitor center to a rock ledge where, if the lake is calm, the mysterious pictographs can be seen. Park interpreters are on-site between 11am and 3pm in July and August, weather permitting.

Avid hikers will delight in the park's 11 exceptional trails. The signature hike is the 65km Coastal Trail, a steep, challenging route along craggy cliffs and pebble beaches (allow five to seven days total). There are six access points, allowing you to spend from a few hours to several days tackling a section of the trail. The Nokomis Trail (5km) loops around iconic Old Woman Bay, so named because it is said you can see the face of an old woman in the cliffs. Depending on the weather, wispy beard-like fog and shivering Arctic trees exude a distinctly primeval flavor. The diverse Orphan Lake Trail (8km) just north of Katherine Cove is a tasting plate of the park's ethereal features: isolated cobble beaches, majestic waterfalls, elevated lookouts and dense maple forests.

There's a burgeoning paddling culture here, with canoes available to rent in the park ($10/30 per hour/day). Several charted inland routes range from the relatively mild 16km Fenton-Treeby Loop (with 11 short portages of 150m each max) to challenging routes accessible only via the Algoma Central Tour Train (p78) if it resumes its passenger services. Naturally Superior Adventures (p31) runs extensive paddling programs in and around the park.

There are two campgrounds close to the highway: Agawa Bay, right on Lake Superior; and Rabbit Blanket Lake, next to an inland lake with less wind and higher temperatures but fewer coastal vistas. Booking through Ontario Parks (www.ontarioparks.com) is essential.

Slate Islands   ISLAND

(📞 807-825-3403; www.ontarioparks.com/park/slateislands) Drop by the town of Terrace Bay (www.terracebay.ca) and catch a boat (return from $165 each with four people) 13km to this outstanding archipelago, which is possibly the remains of an ancient meteorite. The islands are home to snowshoe hare and one of the world's largest herds of woodland caribou, as well as forested inlets for kayaking explorations. Naturally Superior Adventures (p31) runs five-day kayaking expeditions here ($1950).

There are no visitor facilities on the island, and as Slate Islands is crown land, Canadian citizens and residents are allowed to camp up to 21 days free of charge. If you are not a Canadian resident, you are supposed to buy a camping permit at any ServiceOntario government office.

Sleeping Giant Provincial Park   PARK

(📞 807-977-2526; www.ontarioparks.com/park/sleepinggiant; Hwy 587; day use per vehicle $11.25, campsites $37-42, cabins from $170, camping trailers $98-142) Seen across the lake from Thunder Bay, the jagged Sleeping Giant Peninsula resembles a large reclining man. Its rugged, forested terrain has been considered a sacred realm for millennia. The Sleeping Giant Provincial Park covers much of the craggy promontory, offering unforgettable views of Lake Superior.

The park is wild enough to offer backcountry camping and over 80km of hiking trails, yet compact enough for a fulfilling day trip from Thunder Bay, around 70km west. Contact Ontario Parks (www.ontarioparks.com) for reservations. On trails such as the 40km, multiday Kabeyun, which follows the peninsula's dramatic coastline, you might see moose, wolf, fox or lynx in the boreal forest. There are also short trails of 1km and up, and kayak and canoe rental. At the tip of the peninsula, you'll find the remote community of Silver Islet. In the mid-1880s the town exploded with the world's richest silver mine, now abandoned, and was a Hollywood location of choice in the early 20th century.

Thunder Bay

📞 807 / POP 93,952

Thunder Bay is about as comfortably isolated as you can get – it's 706km west of Sault Ste Marie and 703km east of Winnipeg (Manitoba). If you're arriving by road, it's a welcome return to civilization: no matter how beautiful the forests and shoreline, they start to blur together after a few hundred kilometers. With a smattering of historical attractions, surrounding natural beauty, and creative restaurants and bars in its regenerated downtown Entertainment District, you might be pleasantly surprised that Thunder Bay hums along strongly, in defiance and celebration of its long, dark winters. Maybe it has something to do with the fact that 10% of the population are of Finnish descent.

◉ Sights

★ **Fort William Historical Park**   MUSEUM
(📞807-473-2344; www.fwhp.ca; 1350 King Rd; adult/child $14/10; ⊙10am-5pm mid-May–mid-Sep, tours every 45min) French voyageurs, Scottish gentlemen and Ojibwe scuttle about while reenacting life in the early 1800s at this historical park. From 1803 to 1821, Fort William was the headquarters of the North West Company. Eventually the business was absorbed by the Hudson's Bay Company and the region's importance as a trading center declined. Today the large heritage center offers 46 reconstructed historic buildings stuffed with entertaining and antiquated props such as muskets, pelts and birch-bark canoes.

Marina Park   HARBOR
(📞Nov-Apr 807-625-2941, mid-May–mid-Oct 807-345-2741; www.thunderbay.ca/en/recreation/marina. aspx; Sleeping Giant Pkwy) The focus of exciting development plans, Thunder Bay's marina area is a pedestrianized haven of parkland, fountains, footpaths, a skate park and public art. Pick up the free *Public Art Walking Tour Guide,* covering the many installations

along the waterfront, from the tourist offices. Outdoor movies, concerts and festivals take place here in summer.

Bay & Algoma Historical District   AREA
Thunder Bay has a population of well over 10,000 Finnish Canadians, descended from immigrants who began arriving in the late 19th century. Locals happily honor this heritage by taking saunas and eating pancakes. In this historical Finnish district around the intersection of Bay and Algoma Sts, you will see Scandinavian shops and businesses and perhaps hear older people speaking Finnish.

David Thompson
Astronomical Observatory   OBSERVATORY
(📞807-473-2344; www.fwhp.ca/observatory; 1350 King Rd; adult/child $10/8; ⊙10pm-midnight Thu-Sat May-Aug, 9-11pm Thu-Sat Sep & Oct, shorter hours rest of year) Peek at the stars through one of Canada's largest telescopes at Fort William Historical Park's fantastic, accessible observatory. Check the website for the latest viewing conditions. Even if the weather is cloudy, join a Star Walk for a virtual tour of the night sky.

Thunder Bay Museum   MUSEUM
(📞807-623-0801; www.thunderbaymuseum.com; 425 Donald St E; adult/child $3/1.50; ⊙11am-5pm mid-Jun–early Sep, from 1pm Tue-Sun early Sep–mid-Jun) This century-old museum is engaging for adults and children alike. Displays about Ojibwe culture, fur trading, military history and recent developments incorporate well-presented artifacts to offer visitors a glimpse of the region's 10,000 years of human history.

Thunder Bay Art Gallery   GALLERY
(📞807-577-6427; www.theag.ca; 1080 Keewatin St, Confederation College; adult/child under 12yr $5/ free; ⊙noon-8pm Tue-Thu, to 5pm Fri-Sun) Thunder Bay's premier gallery offers an eclectic assortment of contemporary art, including works by indigenous artists from northwestern Ontario and beyond. The painters' use of natural imagery, haunting masks and scorching primary colors will leave a lasting impression on visitors.

Mt McKay   VIEWPOINT
(📞807-623-9543; www.fwfn.com; Mission Rd; per vehicle $5; ⊙9am-10pm mid-May–early Oct) Mt McKay rises 350m over Thunder Bay, offering sweeping views of the region's patchwork of rugged pines and swollen rock formations. The lookout is part of the Fort

Fort William Historical Park

William First Nation reserve, and reveals its most majestic moments in the evening when the valley is but a sea of blinking lights. An easy walking trail ascends 175m from the viewing area to the top of the mountain. Watch your step while climbing – the shale rock can cause tumbles.

🏃 Activities

Sail Superior   BOATING
(☑ 807-628-3333; www.sailsuperior.com; Pier 3, Sleeping Giant Pkwy) Sailboat tours on Lake Superior from Thunder Bay marina, including 1½-hour trips around the harbor (adult/child under 10 years $59/25, minimum four people).

Loch Lomond Ski Area   SKIING
(☑ 807-475-7787; www.lochlomond.ca; 1800 Loch Lomond Rd; full-/half-day lift tickets from $46/34; ⊙ Dec-Apr) With 17 runs, equally distributed between beginner, intermediate and advanced, this is a great hill to learn on and a wonderful place to ski with kids. Skiing and snowboarding equipment rental and lessons are available, and there's also tubing ($15). In summer, the slopes are open to hikers and mountain bikers.

Kangas   HEALTH & FITNESS
(☑ 807-344-6761; www.kangassauna.ca; 379 Oliver Rd; sauna/hot tub hire from $22/20; ⊙ 7:30am-8pm Mon-Fri, from 8am Sat & Sun) Reflecting Thunder Bay's Finnish heritage, this local institution offers 1½-hour private rental of its saunas.

Each accommodates up to six people, so go it alone or grab a 'conference room' for you and your 'associates.' There's also a hot tub, and the cafe (mains $10) is popular for breakfast.

🛏 Sleeping

Most of the big motel chains are represented south of downtown: on Memorial Ave and around the intersections of Hwy 11/17 and the Harbour Expressway, and Hwy 61 and Arthur St W (near the airport). Northeast of downtown, a few independent motels on Cumberland St N/Hodder Ave charge around $70 for a room. It is worth booking ahead, as Thunder Bay's role as a regional hub keeps the hotels busy.

Strathcona Motel   MOTEL **$**
(☑ 807-683-8136; www.strathconamotel.ca; 545 Hodder Ave; d $80; P 🛜) This tiny motel has been in the family since personable owner Ken was a kid. Dating back to 1956, the six self-catering units with separate bedrooms are a veritable time warp, but spotlessly clean and atmospheric. It's a few kilometers east of downtown, in a lovely neighborhood with parks and bike paths.

Thunder Bay International Hostel   HOSTEL **$**
(☑ 807-983-2042; www.thunderbayinternationalhostel. ca; 1594 Lakeshore Dr; campsites $25, d per person $25; P 🛜) Colorful bric-a-brac – including antlers, a baby grand piano and an old bus – lies splayed across the shrubby lawn as

WINNIE THE WHO?

The little logging town of White River (www.whiteriver.ca) lays claim to being the home of the original Winnie the Pooh.

As the story goes, back in 1914, a trapper returned to White River with an orphaned baby black bear cub. A veterinarian soldier named Harry Colebourn was on a rail layover in White River when he came across the trapper and fell in love with the cub, purchasing her for $20. He named her 'Winnipeg.' She boarded the Québec-bound troop train with Harry, en route to his native Britain.

When Harry was called to serve in France, he left Winnie in the care of the London Zoo, where she became an instant hit. One of the many hearts she won over belonged to a young Christopher Robin Milne, son of AA Milne. A frequent visitor to the zoo, young Christopher's pet name for the little bear was 'Winnie-the-Pooh.' In his 1926 first edition, AA Milne noted that his stories were about his son, the bear from the London Zoo, and Christopher's stuffed animals.

Eventually, Disney purchased Milne's tales of Winnie-the-Pooh and Christopher Robin, and...the rest is history. A monument to both bears, actual and fictional, stands in the park in White River, by the visitors center.

though Alice in Wonderland were having a garage sale. Charismatic owner Lloyd champions the backpacking lifestyle; he's a kind-hearted, well-traveled soul who cares about his guests. The hostel is 25km east of town, close to Sleeping Giant Provincial Park.

Prince Arthur Waterfront Hotel & Suites   HOTEL $$
(☑807-345-5411; www.princearthurwaterfront.com; 17 Cumberland St N; d with city/lake view $115/125; P❀@☎☼) Following a renovation, this stately, century-old building is a good option once again. Rooms are spacious, with a distinctly old-fashioned feel. Where the hotel lacks polish, it compensates with its central harborside location and pool, gym, sauna and restaurant – all for the price of a chain motel.

★ **Delta Hotel by Marriott**   HOTEL $$$
(☑807-344-0777; www.marriott.com; 2240 Sleeping Giant Pkwy; d from $239; P❀) Thunder Bay's newest and fanciest hotel, right on the waterfront, is a worthwhile splurge. The rooms are large and full of all amenities, but it's the views over the marina toward the Sleeping Giant that make it worth the price.

🍴 Eating

★ **Hoito Restaurant**   FINNISH $
(☑807-345-6323; www.thehoito.ca; 314 Bay St; mains $9-15; ☺8am-3pm Sun-Thu, to 7pm Fri & Sat) You'll think you've stumbled into a staff cafeteria in Finland; indeed, that's how the Hoito started, over a century ago, providing affordable meals to Finnish workers. This Thunder Bay institution's all-day breakfast

of flattened Finnish *lättyjä* pancakes is the only way to start the day here. It's in the basement of the historic Finnish Labour Temple, now a cultural center.

★ **Prime Gelato**   ICE CREAM $
(☑807-344-1185; www.primegelato.ca; 200 Red River Rd; cup/waffle cone from $4/5.25; ☺2-9pm Wed-Fri, from noon Sat, to 4pm Sun) With ambitions to be a Ben & Jerry's of the north, Prime sells gelato and sorbet in creative flavors such as salted caramel, and sometimes alcoholic options made with Kenora's Lake of the Woods beer. The dozen or so gluten-free creations on offer frequently change, but most incorporate fresh local produce from maple syrup to strawberries.

★ **Tomlin**   CANADIAN $$
(☑807-346-4447; www.tomlinrestaurant.com; 202 Red River Rd; mains $16-28, cocktails $10-14; ☺5-10pm Tue-Sat) 🍴 Locally lauded chef Steve Simpson's elevated comfort food uses seasonal local ingredients, with the regularly changing menu split between small plates (eg beef tartare and smoked cauliflower) and large (veal cavatelli, crab and scallop linguine, redfin trout). The wine list is 100% Ontarian and includes ice wine, while creative cocktails such as the smoked port Manhattan also incorporate local ingredients.

Bight   INTERNATIONAL $$$
(☑807-622-4448; www.bightrestaurant.ca; 2201 Sleeping Giant Pkwy; mains $19-35; ☺11:30am-10pm Sun-Thu, to 11pm Fri & Sat; P☎) At this under-stated marina restaurant, chef Allan Rebelo has created a contemporary menu including charcuterie boards, pizza, fish tacos, and

shrimp and lobster pasta. Sit outside between giant teardrop sculptures, or in the black, white and metal interior.

🍷 Drinking & Nightlife

Head to the Entertainment District, on and around the eastern (lake) end of Red River Rd in the regenerated downtown area, for an excellent selection of restaurants and bars offering live music. Over the pedestrian footbridge from here, Marina Park (p80) hosts outdoor movies, concerts and festivals in summer.

Look out for the locally brewed Sleeping Giant and Dawson Trail craft beers.

★ Sleeping Giant
Brewing Co.   MICROBREWERY
(📋 807-344-5225; www.sleepinggiantbrewing.ca; 712 Macdonell St; ⊘ 11am-10pm Mon-Sat, from noon Sun; 🐾) Established in 2012, this microbrewery was one of the first to take the risk of making different beers in a city known as a 'lager land.' The brewery can be credited with nurturing Thunder Bay's food culture, which has grown under the mantra of local ingredients and local knowledge, something that Sleeping Giant has championed since the beginning.

★ Red Lion Smokehouse   CRAFT BEER
(📋 807-286-0045; www.redlionsmokehouse.ca; 16 Cumberland St S; ⊘ noon-10pm Tue-Thu, from 5pm Mon, to midnight Fri & Sat, to 9pm Sun) Now in a new space a few doors down from its old location, Thunder Bay's favorite hangout is bigger, brighter and has 12 taps of Ontario craft beer and over 100 cans. The food (mains $13 to $20) is just as good as before and the vibe still oozes industrial cool and coziness.

Sovereign Room   BAR
(📋 807-343-9277; www.sovereignroom.com; 220 Red River Rd; ⊘ 4pm-2am Tue-Sat, from 11am Sun) From the chandelier behind the bar to the ornate olive wallpaper, dark woody booths and upward curling staircase by the storefront window, 'the Sov' is an atmospheric spot for a beer. There's live music, and the menu (mains $12 to $20) features staples and surprises such as duck poutine, stone-baked pizza, chicken wings and nachos.

St Paul Roastery   COFFEE
(📋 807-344-3900; 11 St Paul St; ⊘ 7:30am-5pm Mon-Fri, from 9am Sat) Get your fix of black gold at this hip temple to the bean, which doubles as a roastery and has an adjoining record shop.

ℹ️ Information

Pagoda Information Center (📋 807-684-3670; www.tourismthunderbay.com; cnr Red River Rd & Water St; ⊘ 10am-6pm Tue-Sat Jul & Aug) Canada's oldest tourist information bureau, in a distinctive building dating from 1909, remains the city's most central source of visitor information.

Tourism Thunder Bay (📋 800-667-8386, 807-983-2041; www.tourismthunderbay.com; 1000 Hwy 11/17; ⊘ 9am-5pm) The city's largest tourist office is located 6km east of town at the Terry Fox Lookout & Memorial.

Québec's embrace of terroir, its language, its passion for everything from winter snow to wine to gastronomy encompasses identities both distinctly North American and European.

Québec

MONTRÉAL

POP 4.1 MILLION

Historically, Montréal – the only de facto bilingual city on the continent – has been torn right in half, the 'Main' (Blvd St-Laurent) being the dividing line between the east-end Francophones and the west-side Anglos. Today French pockets dot both sides of the map, a new wave of English-speaking Canadians have taken up residence in some formerly French enclaves and, thanks to constant waves of immigration, it's not uncommon for Montréalers to speak not one, or two, but three languages in their daily life. With the new generation concerned more with global issues (namely the environment), language battles have become so passé.

One thing not up for debate is what makes Montréal so irresistible. It's a secret blend of French-inspired joie de vivre and cosmopolitan dynamism that has come together to foster a flourishing arts scene, an indie rock explosion, a medley of world-renowned boutique hotels, the Plateau's extraordinary cache of swank eateries and a cool Parisian vibe that pervades every *terrasse* (patio) in the Quartier Latin. It's easy to imagine you've been transported to a distant locale, where hedonism is the national mandate. Only the

stunning vista of a stereotypical North American skyline from Parc du Mont-Royal's Kondiaronk Lookout will ground you.

Sights

First on most itineraries is Old Montréal, where the heart of the city's history and grandeur can be chased through a labyrinth of winding lanes. Waterfront attractions in the Old Port have benefited immensely from continued rejuvenation, and across the water the attractions and trails of Parc Jean-Drapeau (www.parcjeandrapeau.com; P 🐾; M Jean-Drapeau) 🍃 make a great summer escape from the urban jungle. Downtown encompasses stellar museums and universities, while the bohemian Mile End and Plateau Mont-Royal districts are perfect for meandering and sipping artisanal drinks come evening. The Village and Quartier Latin jolt awake at nighttime. Just outside the city, the Olympic Park, Jardin Botanique and Lachine hold sightseeing appeal. From the panorama at Mont-Royal it's possible to take it all in at once.

★ Basilique Notre-Dame   CHURCH
(📞 846-842-2925; www.basiliquenotredame.ca; 110 Rue Notre-Dame Ouest; adult/child $8/5; ⏰ 8am-4:30pm Mon-Fri, to 4pm Sat, 12:30-4pm Sun; M Place-

d'Armes) Montréal's famous landmark, No-tre Dame Basilica, is a visually pleasing if slightly gaudy symphony of carved wood, paintings, gilded sculptures and stained-glass windows. Built in 1829 on the site of an older and smaller church, it also sports a famous Casavant Frères organ and the Gros Bourdon, said to be the biggest bell in North America. Admission includes an optional 20-minute guided tour in English.

★ Place d'Armes   HISTORIC SITE

(M Place-d'Armes) This open square is framed by some of the finest buildings in Old Mon-tréal, including its oldest bank, first sky-scraper and Basilique Notre-Dame (p84). The square's name references the bloody battles that took place here as religious settlers and indigenous groups clashed over control of what would become Mon-tréal. At its center stands the Monument Maisonneuve, dedicated to city founder Paul de Chomedey, *sieur* de Maisonneuve.

★ Old Port   PARK

(Vieux-Port de Montréal; ⬛) Montréal's Old Port has morphed into a park and fun zone paralleling the mighty St Lawrence River for 2.5km and punctuated by four grand *quais* (quays). Locals and visitors alike come here for strolling, cycling and in-line skating. Cruise boats, ferries, jet boats and speedboats all depart for tours from var-ious docks. In winter you can cut a fine figure on an outdoor ice-skating rink (Parc du Bassin Bonsecours; adult/child $6/4, skate rental $7; ☉10am-9pm Mon-Wed, to 10pm Thu-Sun; ☷14, M Champ-de-Mars).

★ Musée des Beaux-Arts
de Montréal   MUSEUM

(Museum of Fine Arts; www.mbam.qc.ca; 1380 Rue Sherbrooke Ouest; all exhibitions & pavilions adult over 30yr/21-30yr/under 20yr $24/16/free, after 5pm Wed special exhibition $12; ☉10am-5pm Tue-Sun, to 9pm Wed special exhibitions only; M Guy-Concordia) A must for art-lovers, the Museum of Fine Arts has amassed centuries' worth of paintings, sculpture, decorative arts, furniture, prints, drawings and photographs. European heavy-weights include Rembrandt, Picasso and Monet, but the museum really shines when it comes to Canadian art. Highlights include works by Prudence Heward and Paul Kane, landscapes by the Group of Seven and ab-stractions by Martha Townsend and Jean-Paul Riopelle. Temporary exhibits are often exceptional and have included a showcase on French fashion designer Thierry Mugler.

★ Musée McCord   MUSEUM

(McCord Museum of Canadian History; ☏514-861-6701; www.mccord-museum.qc.ca; 690 Rue Sherbrooke Ouest; adult/student/child $20/14/free, special exhibitions extra $5, after 5pm Wed free; ☉10am-6pm Tue, Thu & Fri, to 9pm Wed, to 5pm Sat & Sun; M McGill) With hardly an inch to spare in its cramped but welcoming galleries, the McCord Museum of Canadian History hous-es thousands of artifacts and documents illustrating Canada's social, cultural and ar-chaeological history from the 18th century to the present day, with a small-but-excellent First Nations permanent collection display-ing Indigenous dress and artifacts.

★ Marché Atwater   MARKET

(☏514-937-7754; www.marchespublics-mtl.com; 138 Ave Atwater; ☉7am-6pm Mon-Wed, to 7pm Thu, to 8pm Fri, to 5pm Sat & Sun; M Atwater) 🍴 Just off the Canal de Lachine (p86), this fantas-tic market has a mouthwatering assortment of fresh produce from local farms (some promoting sustainability), excellent wines, crusty breads, fine cheeses and other delec-table fare. The market's specialty shops op-erate year-round, while outdoor eatery stalls open from March to October. It's all housed in a 1933 brick hall, topped with a clock tow-er, and little bouts of live music pop off with pleasing regularity. The grassy banks over-looking the canal are great for a picnic.

★ Biodôme   MUSEUM

(☏514-868-3000; www.espacepourlavie.ca; 4777 Ave du Pierre-De Coubertin; adult/child $20/10; ☉9am-6pm late Jun-Sep, 9am-5pm Tue-Sun rest of year; ⬛; M Viau) At this captivating exhibit you can amble through a rainforest, explore Antarctic islands, view rolling woodlands, take in aquatic life in the Gulf of St Law-rence, or wander along the raw Atlantic oceanfront – all without ever leaving the building. The five ecosystems house many thousands of animal and plant species; fol-low the self-guided circuit and you will see everything. Be sure to dress in layers for

---

ℹ **MONTRÉAL MUSEUM PASS**

Custom-made for culture buffs, this handy pass (www.museesmontreal.org/en/cards/the-passes; 3-day pass $80) is the most cost-effective way to access 41 of Montréal's museums over a three-day period – the price includes unlimited public transportation during this time.

Montréal

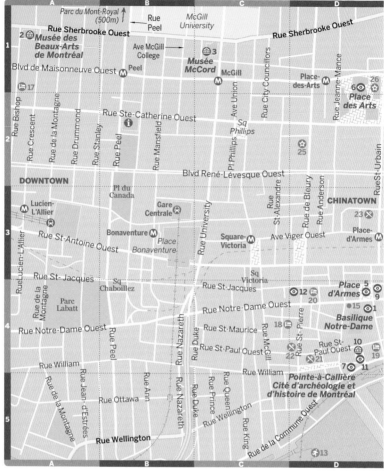

the temperature swings. You can borrow free strollers; and interactive exhibits are at small-child height.

★ Jardin Botanique
GARDENS

(☎ 514-872-1400; www.espacepourlavie.ca/jardin botanique; 4101 Rue Sherbrooke Est; adult/child $21/10; ☺ 9am-6pm mid-May–early Sep, 9am-5pm Tue-Sun early Sep–mid-May; ♿; Ⓜ Pie-IX) 🔗 Montréal's Jardin Botanique is the third-largest botanical garden in the world, after London's Kew Gardens and Berlin's Botanischer Garten. Since its 1931 opening, the 75-hectare garden has grown to include tens of thousands of species in more than 20 thematic gardens, and its wealth of flowering plants

is carefully managed to bloom in stages. The rose beds are a sight to behold in summertime. Climate-controlled greenhouses host cacti, banana trees and 1500 species of orchid. Twitchers should bring their binoculars.

★ Canal de Lachine
CANAL

(Rue Charles-Biddle; ♿ 🚲) 🔗 FREE A perfect marriage of urban infrastructure and green civic planning: a 14km-long cycling and pedestrian pathway, with picnic areas and outdoor spaces. Since the canal was reopened for navigation in 2002, flotillas of pleasure and sightseeing boats glide along its calm waters. Old warehouses converted into luxury condos line the canal near Atwater mar-

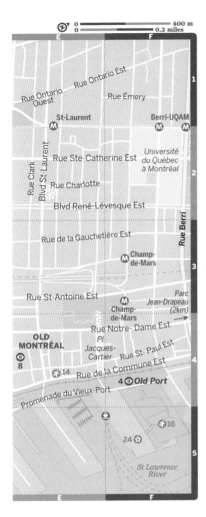

0 0 400 m
0 0.2 miles

Montréal

ket (p85). The Lachine Canal was originally built in 1825 as a means of bypassing the treacherous Lachine Rapids on the St Lawrence River.

★ **Pointe-à-Callière Cité d'archéologie et d'histoire de Montréal**   MUSEUM
(Museum of Archaeology & History; ☑514-872-9150; www.pacmuseum.qc.ca; 350 Pl Royale; adult/child $22/8; ⊗10am-5pm Tue-Fri, from 11am Sat & Sun; ☖; Ⓜ Place-d'Armes) One of Montréal's most fascinating sites, this museum takes visitors on a historical journey through the centuries, beginning with the early days of Montréal. Visitors should start with *Yours Truly, Montréal,* an 18-minute multimedia show that covers the arrival of Indigenous peoples, the founding of Montréal and other key moments. Afterward, head to the archaeological crypt where you can explore the remains of the city's ancient sewage and river system, and the foundations of its first buildings and public square.

🕏 Activities & Tours

Montréal is a cyclist's haven. With Bixi (☑514-789-2494; http://montreal.bixi.com; per 30min $2.95; ⊗24hr mid-Apr–Oct) 🚲, a popular self-service, solar-powered bicycle rental system with over 600 stations, it's easy for anyone to reap the benefits of Montréal's more than 500km of bicycle and skating paths. If you're planning a longer cycling trip, however, you're better off visiting a rental shop for a greater selection of bikes and maps. One popular route parallels the Canal de Lachine for 14.5km, starting in Old Montréal and passing a lot of history en route. Picnic tables are scattered along the way, so pick up some tasty provisions at the fabulous Marché Atwater (p85). The smooth Circuit Gilles Villeneuve (www.parcjeandrapeau.com) on Île Notre-Dame is another cool track. It's open and free to all from mid-April to mid-November – except in mid-June when it hosts the Grand Prix du Canada Formula One car race.

You can rent bikes from Ça Roule Montréal (☑ 514-866-0633; www.caroulemontreal.com; 27 Rue de la Commune Est, Old Port; bikes per hour/day from $9/40, in-line skates 1st/additional hour $9/4; ⊘ 9am-7pm, reduced hours winter; Ⓜ Place-d'Armes).

Bota Bota
SPA

(☑ 514-284-0333; www.botabota.ca; 358 Rue de la Commune Ouest, Old Port; ⊘ 10am-10pm, from 9am Fri-Sun; Ⓜ Square-Victoria) This unique floating spa is actually a 1950s ferry that's been repurposed as an oasis on the water. It's permanently docked by the Old Port with great city views, offering a range of treatments on its five beautifully redesigned decks. Water Circuit admission (from $40) gives you access to saunas, hot tubs and outdoor terraces.

Plage Jean-Doré
BEACH

(Plage des Îles; ☑ 514-872-0199; www.parcjeandrapeau.com; Île Notre-Dame; adult/child $9/4.50; ⊘ 10am-7pm daily mid-Jun–late Aug, noon-7pm Sat-Mon late Aug-early Sep; ⓗ; Ⓜ Jean-Drapeau, then bus 767) On warm summer days this artificial sandy beach on Île Notre-Dame can accommodate up to 5000 sunning and splashing souls. It's safe, clean and ideal for kids; picnic facilities and snack bars serving beer are on-site. There are also paddleboats, canoes and kayaks for rent.

Guidatour
WALKING

(☑ 514-844-4021; www.guidatour.qc.ca; ticket office 360 Rue St-François-Xavier; adult/child $30/17; ⊘ scheduled tours Fri-Sun May & daily Jun-Oct, private tours year-round) In business for more than three decades, the experienced bilingual guides of Guidatour paint a picture of Old Montréal's eventful history with anecdotes and legends. They also offer culinary tours, plus a 'Christmas Secrets of Old Montréal' tour in December.

✲✲ Festivals & Events

★ Festival International de Jazz de Montréal
MUSIC

(www.montrealjazzfest.com; ⊘ late Jun-early Jul) For 10 days the heart of downtown explodes in jazz and blues during 1000 concerts, most of them outdoors and free. This is the world's largest jazz festival, but there's also world music, rock and some pop music.

★ Just for Laughs Festival
COMEDY

(www.hahaha.com; ⊘ mid-Jul) Everyone gets giddy for two weeks at this international comedy festival, the world's largest, with hundreds of stand-up shows, including free ones in the Quartier Latin. Past performers include Tina Fey, Trevor Noah, Laverne Cox and John Mulaney. If you don't know who to see, try a themed multi-comic night, such as 'The Ethnic Show.' Book ahead.

Montréal Pride
LGBTIQ+

(Fierté Montréal; ☑ 514-903-6193; http://fiertemtl.com; ⊘ Aug) Montréal's Pride Week (the largest in Canada and the Francophone world) promotes local LGBTIQ+ communities every August, culminating in the annual Montréal Pride Parade on René-Lévesque Blvd, attracting around 300,000 spectators.

PLACE DES ARTS

• •

Montréal's performing-arts center is the nexus for artistic and cultural events. Several renowned musical companies call Place des Arts (☑ box office 514-842-2112; www.placedesarts.com; 175 Rue Ste-Catherine Ouest; Ⓜ Place-des-Arts) home, including Opéra de Montréal (☑ 514-985-2258; www.operademontreal.com) and the Montréal Symphony Orchestra (OSM; ☑ 514-840-7400; www.osm.ca; 1600 Rue St-Urbain, Maison Symphonique; ⊘ box office 9am-5pm Mon-Fri & 90min before shows), based in the acoustically brilliant 2100-seat Maison Symphonique. It's also center stage for Festival International de Jazz de Montréal. A key part of the Quartier des Spectacles, the complex embraces an outdoor plaza with fountains and an ornamental pool and is attached to the Complexe Desjardins shopping center via an underground tunnel.

PARC DU MONT-ROYAL

Montréalers are proud of their 'mountain,' the work of New York Central Park designer Frederick Law Olmsted. Parc du Mont-Royal (514-843-8240; www.lemontroyal.qc.ca; 1260 Chemin Remembrance; ; Mont-Royal, then bus 11) FREE is a sprawling, leafy playground that's perfect for cycling, jogging, picnicking and, in winter, cross-country skiing, tobogganing and ice-skating on the Lac Aux Castors (free, ice-skate rentals per 2hr $9; 9am-9pm Sun-Thu, to 10pm Fri & Sat, weather permitting; 11). In fine weather, enjoy panoramic views from Kondiaronk Lookout near Chalet du Mont-Royal, a grand old stone villa that hosts big-band concerts in summer, or from Observatoire de l'Est, a favorite rendezvous for lovebirds.

It takes about 30 minutes to walk between the two. En route you'll spot the landmark 40m-high Cross of Montréal (1924), which is illuminated at night. It's there to commemorate city founder Maisonneuve, who single-handedly carried a wooden cross up the mountain in 1643 to give thanks to God for sparing his fledgling village from flooding.

🛏 Sleeping

Montréal's accommodation scene is blessed with a tremendous variety of rooms and styles. Though rates aren't particularly cheap, they are reasonable by international standards – or even compared with other Canadian cities such as Toronto or Vancouver. Reserve at least a month in advance, especially from June to September, for budget accommodations, or to snap up any discounts. French- and Victorian-style inns and independent hotels cater to a variety of budgets.

Auberge Bishop Downtown   HOSTEL $
(514-508-8870; https://aubergebishop.ca; 1447 Rue Bishop; dm $23-30; ; Guy-Concordia) You might never guess that this is a hostel, seeing the winding wooden staircase, stained-glass windows and old French fireplaces in this 1800s brick manor house. Metal beds are comfortable and quiet, though it's worth upgrading for fewer people in the room; it can get cramped in the triple-stacked bunks.

There's a modern white bathroom and shared kitchen.

★ L Hotel   BOUTIQUE HOTEL $$
(514-985-0019; www.lhotelmontreal.com; 262 Rue St-Jacques Ouest; d $219-379; ; Square-Victoria) Inside a grand 1870 building, L Hotel is a major draw for art-lovers. Georges Marciano, founder of Guess jeans, opened the hotel in 2010, showering great artworks throughout the rooms and common areas. You might sleep in a room with an original piece by Andy Warhol, Roy Lichtenstein or Frank Stella, or one of scores of other famed artists.

★ Accueil Chez François   B&B $$
(514-239-4638; www.chezfrancois.ca; 4031 Ave Papineau; s/d from $135/160, with shared bath $115/135; ; Sherbrooke, then bus 24) Overlooking Parc La Fontaine, François indeed gives a warm *accueil* (welcome) to his pleasant and excellent-value five-room guesthouse in the Plateau east. Many guests are repeat visitors, drawn by the spotless and attractive rooms, the delicious breakfasts and the great location (free parking is a bonus).

★ Hôtel Nelligan   BOUTIQUE HOTEL $$$
(514-788-2040, 877-788-2040; www.hotelnelligan. com; 106 Rue St-Paul Ouest; d/ste from $225/360; ; Place-d'Armes) Housed in two restored buildings and named in honor of Québec's famous and tragic poet, Émile Nelligan, this Old Montréal beauty has original details (such as exposed brick or stone) and luxurious fittings (down comforters, high-quality bath products, and Jacuzzis in some rooms).

Verses, a plush bar and restaurant, is next door, with a magnificent roof patio, Terrasse Nelligan.

★ Hôtel Gault   BOUTIQUE HOTEL $$$
(866-904-1616, 514-904-1616; www.hotelgault. com; 449 Rue Ste-Hélène; r from $245; ; Square-Victoria) The Gault delivers beauty and comfort in its 30 spacious rooms. Lovely 19th-century architectural details figure in some rooms, with exposed brick or stone walls, though for the most part it boasts a fashion-forward, contemporary design. Rooms have extremely comfortable beds, ergonomic chairs, high ceilings, huge windows and spotless bathrooms (some with two-person bathtubs) with heated tile floors.

STRETCH YOUR LEGS
MONTRÉAL'S LITTLE BURGUNDY

Start/Finish: Marché Atwater

Distance: 2.4km

Duration: 1½ to 2 hours

Delightful Little Burgundy is made for relaxed strolling. As you walk around this town by a canal, you'll see locals buying fresh produce, cycling for pleasure and eating in casually cool restaurants. You'll also spot enviable converted warehouse homes.

Marché Atwater

The fantastic **Atwater Market** (514-937-7754; www.marchespublics-mtl.com; 138 Ave Atwater; 7am-6pm Mon-Wed, to 7pm Thu, to 8pm Fri, to 5pm Sat & Sun; Atwater) has a mouthwatering assortment of fresh produce from local farms, excellent wines, crusty breads, fine cheeses and other delectable fare. The market's specialty shops operate year-round, while outdoor eatery stalls open from March to October. It's housed in a 1933 brick hall, topped with a clock tower, and little bouts of live music pop off with pleasing regularity. The grassy banks overlooking the Canal de Lachine are great for a picnic with produce from the market.

The Walk >> From the southern exit of the market, walk south 100m to the canal. You'll pass the faux-grass square rest area with picnic tables and a mini-stage for occasional performances. Head west, east or across the bridge to the leafy park – whichever takes your fancy.

Canal de Lachine

A perfect marriage of urban infrastructure and green civic planning, Canal de Lachine incorporates a 14km cycle-and-pedestrian pathway with picnic areas and outdoor spaces. Flotillas of pleasure boats glide along its waters. Old warehouses converted into luxury condos cluster near Atwater Market. If time allows, it's well worth heading out along the canal path on a hired bike or in-line skates from **My Bicyclette** (514-317-6306; www.mybicyclette.com; 2985 Rue St-Patrick; bicycle per 2hr/day from $22/45; 10am-6pm; Charlevoix), or on the water in a kayak or boat, available at nearby **H2O Adventures** (514-842-1306; www.h2oadventures.com; 2727b Rue St-Patrick; pedal boat/tandem kayak/electric boat/voyageur canoe per hr $25/35/50/50; 9am-9pm Jun-Aug, noon-7:30pm Mon-Fri, 10am-7:30pm Sat & Sun Sep-May; Charlevoix).

The Walk >> Cross back by the west side of Marché Atwater along Ave Atwater, passing by a small playground before hitting Rue Notre-Dame

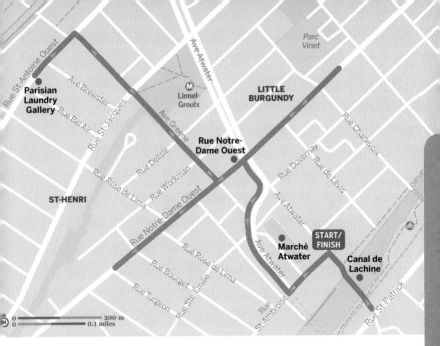

Parc
Vinet

Rue St-Antoine Ouest

Ave Brewster

Parisian
Laundry
Gallery

Rue Bel Air

Rue St-Jacques

Ave Greene

LITTLE
BURGUNDY

Rue Charlevoix

Lionel-
Groulx

Rue Notre-
Dame Ouest

Rue Delisle

Rue Duvernay

Rue de Lévis

ST-HENRI

Rue Rose de Lima

Rue Workman

Ave Atwater

Rue Notre-Dame Ouest

START/
FINISH

Ave Atwater

Marché
Atwater

Canal de
Lachine

Rue Bourget

Rue Rose de Lima

Rue Ste-Émilie

Rue
St-Ambroise

Rue St-Patrick

Rue Turgeon

0   200 m
0   0.1 miles

Ouest after 450m. Look out for street art on the main drag. You'll also spot thrift and antique stores, another local attraction.

Rue Notre-Dame Ouest

Soak up Little Burgundy's alternative/gentrifying vibe with a stroll by its many cafes, restaurants and stores. The pick of the top spots to eat on the street's west side is Asian-retro chic **Satay Brothers** (☎514-933-3507; www.sataybrothers.com; 3721 Rue Notre-Dame Ouest; mains $9-15; ☺11am-11pm Wed-Sun; Ⓜ Lionel-Groulx) for Malaysian *laksa;* to the east, the famous **Joe Beef** (☎514-935-6504; www.joebeef.ca; 2491 Rue Notre-Dame Ouest; mains $30-55; ☺6pm-late Tue-Sat; Ⓜ Lionel-Groulx) restaurants serve a changing selection of hearty Québécois dishes (bookings required). Or head to **Le Bon Vivant** (☎514-316-4585; https://lebv.ca; 2705 Rue Notre-Dame Ouest; mains $15-30; ☺5-11pm Mon-Fri, from 11am Sat & Sun; Ⓜ Lionel-Groulx) for a select menu ranging from grilled octopus or salmon tartare to weekend bagel brunches.

The Walk ❯❯ This 600m walk north from Rue Notre-Dame Ouest along Ave Greene to Parisian Laundry Gallery takes you to the fringes of St-Henri, giving you a peek at the local neighborhood along the way, with its up-down houses, red-brick apartments and converted warehouses.

Parisian Laundry Gallery

A former industrial laundry turned monster gallery (1400 sq meters), this space is worth a trip for the old red-brick building itself, even if you're not a fan of contemporary art. The two (visible) stories of the converted warehouse are seemingly comprised of only windows, some arched, letting in plenty of natural light. Previous exhibitions have included works by New York conceptual artist Adam Pendleton and Québec sculptor Valérie Blass. Be sure to check out exhibits upstairs and in the basement.

The Walk ❯❯ Retrace your steps back south along Ave Greene and Ave Atwater to return to Marché Atwater.

91

✖ Eating

Montréal is one of the great foodie destinations of the North. Here you'll find an outstanding assortment of classic French cuisine, hearty Québécois fare and countless ethnic restaurants from 80-odd nationalities. Today's *haute cuisine* is as likely to be conjured by talented young African, Japanese or Indian chefs as graduates from the Académie Culinaire du Québec.

La Banquise
QUÉBECOIS $

(☑514-525-2415; www.labanquise.com; 994 Rue Rachel Est; mains $8-15; ☺24hr; ⛾; MMont-Royal) A Montréal legend since 1968, La Banquise is probably the best place in town to sample poutine. More than 30 varieties are available, including a vegan poutine, the boogalou (with pulled pork) and straight-up classic poutine. There's an outdoor terrace, a full breakfast menu and a selection of microbrews, plus the kitchen never closes. Expect long lines on weekends.

Fairmount Bagel
BAKERY $

(☑514-272-0667; http://fairmountbagel.com; 74 Ave Fairmount Ouest; bagels $1; ☺24hr; MLaurier) One of Montréal's famed bagel bakeries – people flood in here around the clock to scoop them up the minute they come out of the oven. Classic sesame- or poppy-seed varieties are hits, though everything from cinnamon to all-dressed is here, too. If you want an immediate fix of these honey-water boiled bagels, there is public seating outside.

★ Olive + Gourmando
CAFE $$

(☑514-350-1083; www.oliveetgourmando.com; 351 Rue St-Paul Ouest; mains $11-18; ☺8am-5pm Wed-Sun; ✒; MSquare-Victoria) Named after the owners' two cats, this bakery-cafe is legendary for its hot panini, generous salads and flaky baked goods. Excellent choices include the melted goat's-cheese panini with caramelized onions, decadent mac 'n' cheese, and 'the Cubain' (a ham, roast pork and Gruyère sandwich). Try to avoid the busy lunch rush.

★ Orange Rouge
ASIAN $$

(☑514-861-1116; www.orangerouge.ca; 106 de la Gauchetière Ouest; mains $15-20; ☺11:30am-2:30pm Tue-Fri & 5:30-10:30pm Tue-Sat; MPlace-d'Armes) Hidden down a narrow lane of Chinatown, Orange Rouge has a quaint, low-lit interior that's rather nondescript save for the bright open kitchen at one end and a neon-lit crab sculpture on the wall. Grab a seat at the dark lacquered bar or on one of the banquettes for a feast of Asian fusion.

Le Vin Papillon
INTERNATIONAL $$

(www.vinpapillon.com; 2519 Rue Notre-Dame Ouest; small plates $7-17; ☺3pm-midnight Tue-Sat; ✒; MLionel-Groulx) The folks behind Joe Beef (☑514-935-6504; www.joebeef.ca; 2491 Rue Notre-Dame Ouest; mains $30-55; ☺6pm-late Tue-Sat; MLionel-Groulx) continue the hit parade with this delightful wine bar and small-plate eatery next door to Liverpool House (☑514-313-6049; www.joebeef.ca; 2501 Rue Notre-Dame Ouest; mains $24-50; ☺5-11pm Tue-Sat; ✒) – another Joe Beef success. Creative, mouthwatering veggie dishes take top billing with favorites such as tomato-and-chickpea salad, sautéed chanterelles and smoked-eggplant caviar, plus roasted cauliflower with chicken skin, guinea-fowl confit, and charcuterie platters.

★ Barroco
INTERNATIONAL $$$

(☑514-544-5800; www.barroco.ca; 312 Rue St-Paul Ouest; mains $27-41; ☺5-10:30pm Sun-Wed, to 11pm Thu, to midnight Fri & Sat; MSquare-Victoria) Small, cozy Barroco has stone walls, flickering candles and beautifully presented plates of roast guinea fowl, paella, braised short ribs and grilled fish. The selection is small (just six or so mains and an equal number of appetizers), but you can't go wrong here – particularly if you opt for the outstanding seafood and chorizo paella.

◉ Drinking & Nightlife

Montréalers love a good drink. Maybe it's the European influence: this is a town where it's perfectly acceptable, even expected, to begin cocktail hour after work and continue into the night. Montréal nightlife is the stuff of legend: from underground dance clubs to French hip-hop, dub reggae to breakbeat, comedy shows to supper clubs and indie rock.

★ Crew Café
CAFE

(http://crewcollectivecafe.com; 360 Rue St-Jacques; ☺8am-8pm; ☏; MSquare-Victoria) Easily the most spectacular cafe in Montréal, Crew converted the old Royal Bank into a caffeine and laptop powerhouse. Order from a teller, then sip green tea and good lattes at a gilded deposit-slip (remember those?) and gaze way up at the ornate ceiling laden with chandeliers. It's worth popping in just to have a gander, especially for architecture and interior-design fans.

★ Big in Japan
COCKTAIL BAR

(☑438-380-5658; 4175 Blvd St-Laurent; ☺5pm-3am; MSt-Laurent, then bus 55) Completely concealed from the street, Big in Japan always amazes first-timers. There you are walking along bustling St-Laurent, you find the unmarked door (looking for its small window) by the address, walk down a rather unpromising corridor and emerge into a room lit with a thousand candles (or so it seems). Everything is Japanese-inspired – cocktails, whiskey, beer and bar food.

★ **Barfly** BAR

(📞 514-284-6665; www.facebook.com/BarflyMtl; 4062 Blvd St-Laurent; ⏰ 4pm-3am; Ⓜ St-Laurent, then bus 55) Cheap, gritty, loud, fun and a little bit out of control – just the way we like our dive bars. Live bluegrass and rockabilly bands and bedraggled hipsters hold court alongside aging rockers at this St-Laurent hole-in-the-wall.

★ **La Buvette Chez Simone** WINE BAR

(📞 514-750-6577; www.buvettechezsimone.com; 4869 Ave du Parc; ⏰ 4pm-3am; Ⓜ Laurier) An artsy-chic crowd of (mostly) Francophone bons vivants and professionals loves this cozy wine bar. The staff know their vino and the extensive list is complemented by a gourmet tapas menu. Weekends, the place is jammed from *cinq à sept* (5pm to 7pm 'happy hour') into the wee hours.

☆ Entertainment

Montréal is Canada's unofficial arts capital, with both French and English theater, stand-up comedy, dance, classical and jazz music, and all sorts of interesting blends of the above on stage virtually every night of the week. The city's bilingualism makes it creatively unique and encourages creative collaborations and cross-pollinations that light up the performing-arts scene.

★ **Casa del Popolo** LIVE MUSIC

(📞 514-284-0122; www.casadelpopolo.com; 4873 Blvd St-Laurent; $5-20; ⏰ noon-3am; Ⓜ Laurier) One of Montréal's most charming live venues, the 'House of the People' has talented DJs and is a venue for art-house films and spoken-word performances. It is also known for its vegetarian sandwiches and salads, and is associated with the tapas bar La Sala Rosa (📞 514-844-4227; www.facebook.com/lasalarosa; 4848 Blvd St-Laurent; mains $13-17; ⏰ 5-11pm Tue & Wed, to 2am Thu-Sat, to 10pm Sun; 🍴; Ⓜ Laurier) and its concert venue La Sala Rossa.

Gesù JAZZ

(📞 514-861-4378; www.legesu.com; 1200 Rue de Bleury; shows $18-57; ⏰ box office noon-6:30pm Tue-Sat) This small live-music and events venue

in the basement of a church is blessed with character. Its Greek-theater acoustics means you can see and hear well from any seat. The religious setting has no bearing on performances, which include stand-up comedy, jazz, kids' shows, and even the Montréal Gay Men's Chorus.

★ **Cirque du Soleil** THEATER

(www.cirquedusoleil.com; Quai Jacques-Cartier; tickets from $67; Ⓜ Champ-de-Mars) Globally famous Cirque du Soleil, one of the city's most famous exports, puts on a new production of acrobats and music in this marvelous tent complex every two years or so in summer. These shows rarely disappoint, so don't pass up a chance to see one on its home turf.

★ **Cabaret Mado** CABARET

(📞 514-525-7566; www.mado.qc.ca; 1115 Rue Ste-Catherine Est; tickets $5-15; ⏰ 4pm-3am Tue-Sun; Ⓜ Beaudry) Mado is a flamboyant celebrity who has been featured in *Fugues,* the gay entertainment mag. Her cabaret is a local institution, with drag shows featuring an assortment of hilariously sarcastic performers in eye-popping costumes. Shows take place Tuesday, Thursday and weekend nights; check the website for details.

🛍 Shopping

Style is synonymous with Montréal living. The city itself is beautiful and locals live up to the standard it sets. Maybe it's that much-touted European influence, but most Montréalers seem to instinctively lead stylish lives regardless of income level, enjoying aesthetic pleasures such as food, art and, of course, fashion. Head downtown for budget fashion, to the Plateau and Mile End for cute gift stores and vintage clothing, and the markets for foodie gifts.

★ **Drawn & Quarterly** BOOKS

(📞 514-279-2224; http://mtl.drawnandquarterly.com; 211 Rue Bernard Ouest; ⏰ 10am-8pm; Ⓜ Outremont) The flagship store of this cult independent comic-book and graphic-novel publisher has become something of a local literary haven. Cool book launches take place here, and the quaint little shop sells all sorts of reading matter, including children's books, vintage Tintin comics, recent fiction and art books.

★ **Monastiraki** VINTAGE

(📞 514-278-4879; www.monastiraki.blogspot.ca; 5478 Blvd St-Laurent; ⏰ noon-6pm Wed, to 8pm Thu & Fri, to 5pm Sat & Sun; Ⓜ Laurier) This unclassifiable store named after a flea-market

Place des Artes (p88)

neighborhood in Athens calls itself a 'hybrid curiosity shop/art space,' but that doesn't do justice to what illustrator Billy Mavreas sells: 1960s comic books, contemporary zines, silk-screen posters, and myriad antique and collectible knickknacks, as well as recent works mainly by local graphic artists.

Le Marché des Saveurs du Québec   FOOD & DRINKS
(📞514-271-3811;   www.lemarchedessaveurs.com; 280 Pl du Marché-du-Nord; ⊗9am-6pm Sat-Wed, to 8pm Thu & Fri; Ⓜ Jean-Talon) Everything here is Québécois, from the food to the handmade soaps to a fine collection of artisanal local beer, maple products, jams and cheeses. The store was established so local producers could gain wider exposure for their regional products, and it's a joy to browse.

❶ Information

Centre Infotouriste Montréal (📞514-844-5400; www.mtl.org; 1255 Rue Peel; ⊗9am-6pm May-Sep, to 5pm Oct-Apr; Ⓜ Peel) Information about Montréal and all of Québec. Free hotel, tour and car bookings, plus currency exchange.

EMERGENCY

Montréal Police Station (📞emergencies 911, nonemergencies 514-280-2222)

MEDIA

Magazines The online alternative magazines *Cult* (www.cultmtl.com) and *Hour Community* (www.hour.ca) are even better sources of what's-on listings.

Blogs *MTL Blog* (www.mtlblog.com) is great for up-to-date listings and lots of listicles.

Newspapers The *Montréal Gazette* (www.montrealgazette.com) is the main English-language daily newspaper. The Saturday edition has useful what's-on listings.

EASTERN TOWNSHIPS

Lush rolling hills, crystal-clear lakes and checkerboard farms fill the Eastern Townships, or the Cantons-des-l'Est as they're known by French-speaking inhabitants. The region begins 80km southeast of Montréal and is squished between the labyrinth of minor highways that stretch all the way to the Vermont and New Hampshire borders. New Englanders will feel right at home: covered bridges and round barns dot the bumpy landscape, which is sculpted by the tail end of the US Appalachian mountain range. A visit during spring is rewarding, as it's the season for 'sugaring off' – the tapping, boiling and preparation of maple syrup. In fall the foliage puts on a kaleidoscopic show of colors, to be toasted with freshly brewed apple cider, served in local pubs. The district is also home to a fast-growing wine region that produces some respectable whites and an excellent ice wine – a dessert wine made from frozen grapes. Summer brings fishing and swimming in the region's numerous lakes, and cycling is also extremely popular in the warmer months, with nearly 500km of trails taking in sumptuous landscapes. Winter means excellent downhill skiing at the three main ski hills: Bromont, Mont Orford and Sutton. At Bromont is Gaïa Resto Végan (☑ 450-534-2074; www.legaia.ca; 840 Rue Shefford; mains $9-15; ☺ 8am-3pm Thu-Mon, also 5-8pm Fri & Sat; ✍), easily the culinary draw-card for vegans in the Eastern Townships. Middle Eastern, South Asian and Québécois flavors go into knockout crepes, burgers, bowls and smoothies pretty enough to elic-it 'oohs' and 'aahs' when served up. Details like cashew ricotta elevate fresh ingredients to gourmet dishes great enough to convince an omnivore, and staff have a local warmth. Reservations recommended.

ⓘ Information

Tourist office (Maison du Tourisme des Cantons-de-l'Est; ☑ 450-375-8774; www. easterntownships.org; 100 Rue du Tourisme, Hwy 10, exit 68, St-Alphonse-de-Granby; ☺ 8:30am-6pm Jun-Aug, reduced hours May, Sep & Oct) Produces an excellent cycle-routes map, de-scribing more than a dozen cycling itineraries.

Lac Brome

A stroll around the cute downtown of Lac Brome, which teems with quality boutiques, art galleries, cafes and restaurants, is a fun way to spend an hour or two. Lac Brome is the name given to what is in fact seven amal-gamated villages orbiting the eponymous lake, with Knowlton on the southern shore being the largest, most attractive village and considered its 'downtown.' Although there is evidence of early habitation by Abenaki peo-ples, the area was first formally settled by Loyalists in 1802 and the town still retains an upmarket British flair and numerous 19th-century buildings.

Musée Historique du Comté de Brome   MUSEUM
(☑ 450-243-6782; www.bromemuseum.com; 130 Rue Lakeside, Knowlton; adult/child $8/2; ☺ 10am-5pm; Ⓟ ♿) The exhibits here include a recre-ated general store and courthouse (Sunday only) and, incongruously, a WWI Fokker D-VII plane. An on-site, heavily interactive children's museum is nice for young kids.

Auberge Knowlton   HISTORIC HOTEL $$
(☑ 450-242-6886; www.aubergeknowlton.ca; 286 Chemin Knowlton, Knowlton; d incl breakfast from $168; ✆) Set in a landmark 1849 inn, this place features comfortable country-themed rooms and a sprinkling of antiques through-out. The pleasant on-site restaurant Le Relais serves regional specialties. Breakfast is à la carte.

Le Relais   FRENCH $$
(☑ 450-242-2232; www.aubergeknowlton.ca/relais; 286 Chemin Knowlton, Knowlton; lunch $12-21, dinner $14-35; ☺ 11am-3pm & 5-10pm Mon-Fri, 8am-10pm Sat; ✆) At Auberge Knowlton, this restau-rant features juicy Lac Brome duck served many ways, such as duck ravioli in mush-room sauce, duck confit in orange sauce and duck livers with blackened butter. The many other options include pork tender-loin with calvados, veal piccata and garlic scampi, along with burgers, salads, soups and pasta. Guests of the hotel get a 10% discount.

ⓘ Information

Lac Brome Welcome Centre (☑ 450-243-1221; http://tourismelacbrome.com; 696 Chemin Lakeside; ☺ 9am-5pm mid-Jun-Aug, 10am-6pm Sat & Sun only Sep, Oct & mid-May–mid-Jun) Helpful bilingual staff can set you up with accommodations and maps.

Sutton

Sutton is a little Loyalist town with a pret-ty main street where you can shop to your heart's content or let your hair down dur-ing après-ski partying – the ski area Mont Sutton (☑ 450-538-2545; www.montsutton. com; 671 Rue Maple; day tickets adult/child $68/38; ☺ 9am-4pm; ♿) is nearby. One of southern Québec's most attractive villages, Sutton is popular with artsy types, who come to ap-preciate the scenic beauty of the surround-ing landscape, dominated by the northern Green Mountains. The downtown strip is filled with cafes, restaurants, inns and B&Bs, along with a helpful tourist office (p96).

One of the province's oldest and best-known wine producers, Vignoble l'Orpail-leur is a 30-minute drive from Sutton. Tours of the vineyards are offered, and lunch is served at Le Tire-Bouchon (☑ 450-295-3335; www.orpailleur.ca; 1086 Rue Bruce, Dunham; mains $19-35; ☺ 11:30am-4pm late Jun–mid Oct; ✍), the great little on-site restaurant.

Parc d'Environnement Naturel   HIKING
(☑ 450-538-4085; www.parcsutton.com; adult/child $6/3; ☺ Jun-Oct; ♿) ✎ In summer, Sutton is prime hiking territory, especially in this

conservation area, where 80km of trails have been carved through the thickly forested mountains. Backpackers can unfold their tents at three primitive campgrounds (the one at Lac Spruce is the nicest).

★ **Le Pleasant Hôtel & Café** HISTORIC HOTEL $$
(☑ 450-538-6188; www.lepleasant.com; 1 Rue Pleasant; r $125-259; ❄ @ ☎) This luxurious inn is a great place for a weekend escape or romantic interlude. Some of the sleek and modern rooms – well balanced by a classically historical facade – have views of Mont Sutton (p95), and the breakfasts are memorable.

ℹ Information

Sutton Visitor Information Center (☑ 450-538-8455; https://tourismesutton.ca; 24a Rue Principale Sud; ☉ 11am-4pm, from 10am Fri, to 5pm Sat & Sun) Tourism info for the Sutton area.

Magog

Sitting pretty at the north side of the largest lake in the Eastern Townships, Magog flaunts its beauty with million-dollar waterfront properties, a pretty main street and plenty of decent restaurants and hotels. Magog lies at the confluence of the Magog River, Rivière aux Cerises and Lac Memphrémagog, a banana-shaped lake that stretches south for 44km, all the way across the US border, so visitors are rewarded with sparkling water vistas at every turn.

There's a beach in Magog, but in summer carving out space for your towel can be a tall order. The rest of the shore is largely in private hands, so the lake is best explored from the water with companies such as water-sports outfitter Club de Voile (☑ 819-847-3181; www.voilememphremagog.com; 155 Chemin de la Plage des Cantons; ☉ 9am-5pm Sat & Sun May & Sep, 9am-6pm daily Jun-Aug) and Croisières Escapades Memphrémagog (☑ 819-843-7000; www.escapadesmemphremagog.com; adult $38-108, child $17-72; ☉ Jun-Oct; ⛴), which offers narrated cruises. Watch for Memphré, the elusive creature that lives, Nessie-style, in the lake!

★ **Abbaye St-Benoît-du-Lac** MONASTERY
(☑ 819-843-4080; www.abbaye.ca; 1 Rue Principale, St-Benoît-du-Lac; ☉ church 5am-8:30pm, shop 9-10:45am & 11:45am-6pm Mon-Sat) Sitting on the western shore of Lac Memphrémagog, about 12km south of Magog, this complex is a striking blend of traditional and modern architecture, including a hallway awash in colorful

tiles and a lofty church with exposed structural beams and brick walls. If you can, visit at 7:30am, 11am or 5pm, when the monks practice Gregorian chanting. And check out the monks' apple cider and finely made cheeses, available from the abbey's shop.

À L'Ancestrale B&B B&B $$
(☑ 819-847-5555; www.ancestrale.com; 200 Rue Abbott; r incl breakfast $109-139; @ ☎) Wake up to a five-course gourmet breakfast at this intimate retreat. The five rooms are dressed in a romantic, countrified way and outfitted with refrigerators and coffeemakers. It's central but on a quiet street.

Ô Bois Dormant B&B $$
(☑ 819-843-0450, 888-843-0450; www.oboisdormant.qc.ca; 205 Rue Abbott, Magog; r incl breakfast $130-145; ❄ @ ☎ ⛵) Although only a short walk from the main street, the rambling back lawn at this towering Victorian feels like a secluded resort (the pool helps in this regard). Rooms are cozy, if a little on the chintzy side.

Fondissimo SWISS $$$
(☑ 819-843-8999; 276 Rue Principale Est; mains $26-34; ☉ 5-10pm Jul & Aug, Thu-Sun only rest of year) With a name like Fondissimo, it's not hard to guess the specialty of this hip restaurant in an old renovated factory – there are eight varieties of Swiss fondue alone. Chinese fondue – meat, veggies and seafood, and a piping-hot vat of oil in which to cook it yourself – is also a popular choice.

ℹ Information

Tourist Office (☑ 819-843-2744; www.tourisme-memphremagog.com; 2911 Chemin Milletta; ☉ 9am-5pm, to 6pm late Jun-Aug) Off Rte 115.

Parc National du Mont Orford

There's probably a better summer day than one spent in golden sunshine amid lush green foothills, cool blue lakes and spectacular viewpoints that take in all of the above, but we haven't found it yet. In the meantime, we'll happily show allegiance to Parc National du Mont Orford (☑ 819-843-9855; www.sepaq.com/pq/mor; 3321 Chemin du Parc, Orford; adult/child $8.75/free, parking $8.50; ℗ ⛺), home to snapping turtles, day-tripping families, countless bird species, and hiking, kayaking and canoeing opportunities. It's fairly compact, and often gets busy given its proximity to Magog, which dwarfs the quaint Orford township.

Station de Ski Mont-Orford
SKIING

(☑ 819-843-6548; www.orford.com; 4380 Chemin du Parc; lift tickets per day adult/child $64/37) Station de Ski Mont-Orford has a vertical drop of 589m and dozens of downhill ski slopes, mostly aimed at beginner and intermediate skiers. There's also a snow park with a half-pipe and other fun features.

North Hatley

All of the Eastern Townships are cute, but North Hatley is the geographic equivalent of a yawning puppy. It occupies an enchanting spot at the northern tip of the crystal-clear Lac Massawippi, about 17km east of Magog. This was a popular second home for wealthy US citizens who enjoyed the scenery – and the absence of Prohibition – during the 1920s. Many historic residences have been converted into inns and B&Bs. Popular summer activities include swimming, boating, admiring the lakeshore's natural beauty, and browsing the village's galleries, and antique and craft shops.

There are a few B&Bs and midrange hotels in North Hatley, but a lovely mansion, Manoir Hovey), is the cream of the accommodations crop.

Randonées Jacques Robidas
HORSEBACK RIDING

(☑ 819-563-0166; www.equitationjacquesrobidas.com; 32 Chemin McFarland; riding from $67, 2-day packages from $299; ⊞) A great way to explore the rolling countryside surrounding North Hatley is on horseback with this professional outfit. Among its wide slate of horse-trekking activities, there are welcoming classes for those who are new to the experience.

Manoir Hovey
RESORT $$$

(☑ 819-842-2421; www.manoirhovey.com; 575 Rue Hovey; d from $300, dinner & breakfast incl from $505; ⛛❄@🞉🞈) This lovely resort offers handsomely set rooms in a picturesque lakeside setting. You'll find expansive gardens, a heated pool and an ice rink (in winter), and you can arrange numerous outdoor activities – windsurfing, lake cruises and golfing. The award-winning restaurant Le Hatley is among the best in the Eastern Townships, with four-course meals highlighting refined Québécois fare ($80 for nonguests).

Pilsen
PUB FOOD $$

(☑ 819-842-2971; www.pilsen.ca; 55 Rue Main; mains $17-39, set meals from $35; ⊙ 11:30am-11pm; ⛛) The liveliest restaurant in North Hatley is famous for its salmon, both grilled and smoked, and upmarket pub fare. There's a riverside terrace and another facing the lake.

★ Auberge Le Coeur d'Or
QUÉBÉCOIS $$$

(☑ 819-842-4363; www.aubergelecoeurdor.com; 85 Rue School; 4-course meal $47; ⊙ 6-9pm, closed Mon & Tue Nov-Apr) For a delightful night out, head to this charming farmhouse inn. The restaurant's four- to five-course dinners make abundant use of local ingredients, including cheeses from Sherbrooke, rabbit from Stanstead, duck from Orford and smoked trout from East Hereford. Save room for profiteroles, chocolate mousse cake or the Coeur d'Or's trademark trio of crème brûlées.

Piggery Theatre
THEATER

(☑ 819-842-2431; www.piggery.com; 215 Chemin Simard) In summer, this popular theater stages English-language dramas, concerts and comedy acts.

Sherbrooke

Sherbrooke is the commercial center of the area, a bustling city that's perfect for refueling on modern conveniences before returning to the Eastern Townships. The historic center, 'Vieux Sherbrooke,' sits at the confluence of two rivers and is bisected by Rue Wellington and Rue King, the main commercial arteries. Highlights include the city's small but well-conceived Musée des Beaux-Arts (☑ 619-821-2115; http://mbas.qc.ca; 241 Rue Dufferin; adult/student $10/7; ⊙ 10am-5pm Jul & Aug, noon-5pm Tue-Sun Sep-Jun), with works by Québécois and Canadian artists, and the 18km Réseau Riverain walking and cycling path along the Rivière Magog, which starts at Blanchard Park, west of downtown.

Lac des Nations
LAKE

(⛲) 🏊 South of all the sights, Rivière Magog flows into the pretty Lac des Nations, which is surrounded by a scenic paved trail perfect for walking, in-line skating and cycling (rentals available).

Hotel Le Floral
HOTEL $$

(☑ 819-564-6812; www.hotellefloral.com; 1920 12e Ave Nord; r incl breakfast from $110; ⛛❄🞉🞈) The best of a bunch of midrange options, Le Floral has modish, urban-chic rooms and friendly service; 5km northeast of Sherbrooke.

Au Coin du Vietnam   VIETNAMESE $$
(☑ 819-566-8383; www.aucoinduvietnam.com; 1530 Rue Galt Ouest; set meals from $25; ⊙ 11am-2pm & 5-9pm, closed Mon lunch) If you need a break from Canadian/Québécois cuisine, hit up Au Coin du Vietnam, which dishes out excellent, fresh Southeast Asian fare – steamed rice, grilled pork, curry chicken, crispy noodles and plump prawns.

Siboire   MICROBREWERY
(☑ 819-565-3636; www.siboire.ca; 80 Rue du Dépôt; ⊙ 6am-3am Mon-Fri, from 7:30am Sat & Sun) Sherbrooke's historic train depot houses this atmospheric microbrewery with nearly a dozen beers on tap, including Siboire's own IPA, wheat beer, oatmeal stout, Irish red ale and seasonal maple scotch ale. High ceilings, brick walls and a flower-fringed summer terrace create an inviting atmosphere for drinking everything in and enjoying some of the tastiest fish-and-chips in the Townships.

❶ Information

ATMs are ubiquitous across the town center.

Banque Nationale (3075 Blvd Portland; ⊙ 10am-3pm Mon-Wed & Sat, to 6pm Thu, to 4pm Fri) Fee-free ATM for many foreign cards.

Hospital Hôtel-Dieu (☑ 819-346-1110; www.santeestrie.qc.ca; 580 Rue Bowen Sud; ⊙ 24hr) Local hospital offering a wide range of services.

Tourism Eastern Townships (☑ 819-820-2020, 800-355-5755; www.easterntownships.org; 20 Rue Don-Bosco Sud; ⊙ 8:30am-4:30pm Mon-Fri)

Tourist Office (Destination Sherbrooke; ☑ 819-821-1919; www.destinationsherbrooke.com; 785 Rue King Ouest; ⊙ 9am-5pm, to 3pm Sun)

ZAP Sherbrooke (www.zapsherbrooke.org) Has a list of free wi-fi zones in Sherbrooke.

QUÉBEC CITY

POP 542,045

Québec, North America's only walled city north of Mexico City, is the kind of place that crops up in trivia questions. Over the centuries, the lanes and squares of the Old Town – a World Heritage site – have seen the continent's first parish church, first museum, first stone church, first Anglican cathedral, first girls' school, first business district and first French-language university. Most of these institutions remain in some form. The historical superlatives are inescapable: flick through the *Québec Chronicle-Telegraph* and you're reading North America's oldest newspaper; if you have to visit L'Hôtel-Dieu

de Québec, console yourself with the thought that it's the continent's oldest hospital. Once past Le Château Frontenac, the most photographed hotel in the world, you'll find yourself torn between the various neighborhoods' diverse charms. In Old Upper Town, the historical hub, many excellent museums and restaurants hide among the tacky fleur-de-lis T-shirt stores. Old Lower Town, at the base of the steep cliffs, is a labyrinth, where it's a pleasure to get lost among street performers and cozy inns before emerging on the north shore of the St Lawrence. Leaving the walled town near the star-shaped Citadelle, hip St-Jean-Baptiste is one of the less historical but still interesting areas, and the epicenter of a vibrant nightlife.

◉ Sights

Most of Québec City's sights are found within the compact cluster of Old Town walls, or just outside them, making this a dream destination for pedestrians.

Sandwiched between the Old Upper Town and the waterfront, the Old Lower Town area has the city's most intriguing museums, plus numerous plaques and statues, and plenty of outdoor cafes and restaurants along its pedestrian-friendly streets. Street performers in period costume help recapture life in distant centuries.

Teeming Rue du Petit-Champlain forms the heart of the Quartier Petit-Champlain, the continent's oldest commercial district. Look for the incredible wall paintings that feature on the 17th- and 18th-century buildings. From the Upper Town, you can reach the Lower Town in several ways. Walk down Côte de la Canoterie from Rue des Remparts to the Vieux-Port or edge down the charming and steep Rue Côte de la Montagne. About halfway down on the right there is a shortcut, the Escalier Casse-Cou (Break-Neck Stairs), which leads down to Rue du Petit-Champlain. You can also take the funicular.

⭐ Le Château Frontenac   HISTORIC BUILDING
(☑ 418-692-3861; www.fairmont.com/frontenac-quebec; 1 Rue des Carrières, Old Upper Town) Reputedly the world's most photographed hotel, this audaciously elegant structure was opened in 1893 by the Canadian Pacific Railway as part of its chain of luxury hotels. Its fabulous turrets, winding hallways and imposing wings graciously complement its dramatic location atop Cap Diamant, a cliff that cascades into the raging St Lawrence River. Over the years, it's lured a never-

ending lineup of luminaries, including Alfred Hitchcock, who chose this setting for the opening scene of his 1953 mystery *I Confess*.

★ **Le Monastère des Augustines** MUSEUM
(☑ 418-694-1639; https://monastere.ca; 77 Rue des Remparts, Old Upper Town; adult/youth/child $10.50/4.50/free, guided tour $15/9/free; ☺ 10am-5pm late Jun-Aug, Tue-Sun only Sep-late Jun) On no account should you miss this museum, which traces the history of the order of Augustinian nuns who founded Québec's first hospital, the Hôtel-Dieu, in 1644 and ran it for over 300 years. OK, it may not sound like a crowd-pleaser, but the half-dozen rooms around a central cloister are filled with remarkable displays of religious items, crafts (artificial flowers were mandatory where flowers bloom only four months a year), an old apothecary and an 18th-century refectory.

★ **Terrasse Dufferin** PARK
(Rue des Carrières, Old Upper Town) Perched on a clifftop 60m above the St Lawrence River, this 425m-long boardwalk is a marvelous setting for a stroll, with spectacular, sweeping views. In summer it's peppered with street performers; in winter it hosts a dramatic toboggan run.

Near the statue of Samuel de Champlain, stairways descend to the excavations of Champlain's second fort (☑ 418-648-7016; www.pc.gc.ca/eng/lhn-nhs/qc/saintlouisforts/index.aspx; adult/child $4/free, incl guided tour $15/10; ☺ 9am-5:30pm mid-May–early Oct) ✐, which stood here from 1620 to 1635. Nearby, you can take the funicular (www.funiculaire-quebec.com; Rue du Petit-Champlain; one way $3.50; ☺ 7:30am-10:30pm, to 11:30pm summer) to the Old Lower Town.

★ **Battlefields Park** HISTORIC SITE
(Parc des Champs-de-Bataille; ☑ 418-649-6157; www.theplainsofabraham.ca; Ave George VI, Montcalm & Colline Parlementaire; ☺ 9am-5:30pm; 🚻) ✐ One of Québec City's must-sees, this verdant clifftop park contains the Plains of Abraham, site of the infamous 1759 battle between British General James Wolfe and French General Louis-Joseph Montcalm that determined the fate of the North American continent. Packed with old cannons, monuments and Martello towers, it's a favorite local spot for picnicking, running, skating, skiing and snowshoeing, along with Winter Carnival festivities and open-air summer concerts. For information and to learn more, visit the Musée des Plaines d'Abraham (Plains of Abraham Museum; ☑ 418-649-6157; www.theplainsofabraham.ca; 835

Ave Wilfrid-Laurier, Montcalm & Colline Parlementaire; adult/youth/child $12.25/10.25/4, incl Abraham's bus tour & Martello Tower 1 Jul-early Sep $15.25/11.25/5; ☺ 9am-5:30pm).

★ **Musée de la Civilisation** MUSEUM
(Museum of Civilization; ☑ 418-643-2158; www.mcq.org/en; 85 Rue Dalhousie, Old Lower Town & Port; adult/teen/child $17/6/free, with temporary exhibitions $22/7/free; ☺ 10am-5pm mid-Jun–early Sep, closed Mon early Sep–mid-Jun) This world-class museum wows even before you've clapped your eyes on the exhibits. It is a fascinating mix of modern design that incorporates preexisting buildings with contemporary architecture. The permanent exhibits – 'People of Québec: Then and Now' and 'This Is Our Story' on the province's Indigenous peoples today – are unique, sensitively curated and highly educational, with some clever interactive elements. At any given moment there's an outstanding variety of rotating shows.

St-Jean-Baptiste AREA
Strolling along Rue St-Jean is a great way to feel the pulse of this bohemian district. The first thing that strikes you, once you've recovered from crossing busy Ave Honoré Mercier, is the area's down-to-earth ambience. Good restaurants, interesting shops and hip cafes and bars, many catering to a gay clientele, line the thoroughfare as far as Ave Turnbull. Take any side street and walk downhill (north) to the narrow residential streets like Rue d'Aiguillon, Rue Richelieu and Rue St-Olivier.

La Citadelle FORT
(☑ 418-694-2815; www.lacitadelle.qc.ca; Côte de la Citadelle, Old Upper Town; adult/child $16/6; ☺ 9am-5pm May-Oct, 10am-4pm Nov-Apr) Covering 2.3 sq km, North America's largest fort was begun by the French in the 1750s but what we see today was constructed by the British over 30 years from 1820 and meant to defend the city against an American invasion that never came. A one-hour guided tour takes in numerous historical structures, including the King's Bastion and the reduit used later as a military prison. Visit the museum dedicated to the Royal 22e Régiment on your own afterward.

Musée National des Beaux-Arts du Québec MUSEUM
(Québec National Museum of Fine Arts; ☑ 418-643-2150; www.mnbaq.org; 179 Grande Allée Ouest, Plains of Abraham; adult/youth/child $20/11/free; ☺ 10am-6pm Jun-Aug, to 5pm Tue-Sun Sep-May, to

STRETCH YOUR LEGS
QUÉBEC CITY'S OLD TOWN

Start/Finish: Porte St-Louis

Distance: 3km

Duration: 2 hours

This historical walking tour encompasses a mix of well-known and lesser-known attractions and sights in Vieux-Québec, the city's attractive Old Town. Set off early, before the tour buses arrive.

Porte St-Louis

Begin at **Porte St-Louis** (Rue St-Louis, Old Upper Town), an impressive gate first erected in 1693, which is also an entrance to the **Fortifications of Québec National Historic Site** (www.pc.gc.ca/eng/lhn-nhs/qc/fortifications/index.aspx; 2 Rue d'Auteuil). At the corner of Rue St-Louis and Rue du Corps-de-Garde, a cannon-ball sits embedded in a tree at the base (allegedly since 1759).

The Walk » The walk is a straightforward 320m-long stroll from Porte St-Louis to where Rue St-Louis meets Rue du Corps-de-Garde.

Ursulines Chapel & Museum

At 34 Rue St-Louis, a traditional house dating to 1676 contains the long-established Québécois restaurant **Aux Anciens Canadiens** (www.auxanciens canadiens.qc.ca). The restaurant's steeply pitched roof was typical of 17th-century French architecture. Along adjoining Rue des Jardins you'll pass the **Ursulines Chapel** (www.museedes ursulines.com; 12 Rue Donnacona; ☺10:30am-noon & 1-4:30pm Tue-Sun May-Oct, 1-4:30pm Sat & Sun Nov-Apr), with the finest woodcarving in Québec and where French General Louis-Joseph Montcalm lay from the time of his death in 1759 until 2001. Across from the chapel is the **Ursulines Museum** (www.poleculturedesursulines.ca; 10 Rue Donnacona; adult/youth/child $10/5/free; ☺10am-5pm Tue-Sun May-Sep, 1-5pm Tue-Sun Oct-Apr) in the convent where generations of nuns educated both French and Indigenous girls, starting in 1641.

The Walk » From the Ursulines Museum, walk north along Rue des Jardins then turn left (west) onto Rue Ste-Anne (210m).

Édifice Price

On Rue Ste-Anne is the elegant 1870 **Hôtel Clarendon** (www.hotelclarendon.com; 57 Rue Ste-Anne), Québec City's oldest hotel. Just next door is **Édifice Price** (Price Building; www.ivanhoecambridge.com/en/office-buildings/properties/edifice-price; 65 Rue Ste-Anne), one of Canada's first skyscrapers, built in 1929 for $1 million. Enter

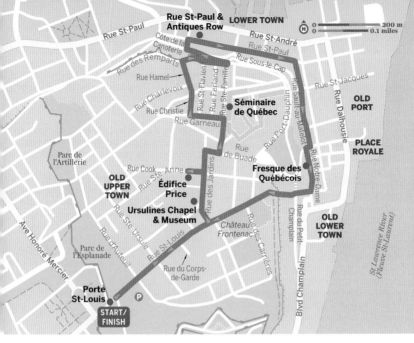

for a look at the art-deco lobby with its fine bronze friezes of loggers at work as well as the stunning coffered ceiling and its brass chandeliers.

The Walk >> A short stroll along Rue des Jardins and then Rue de Buade brings you face-to-face with the heavily restored Basilique-Cathédrale Notre-Dame-de-Québec, which dates in its present form from 1925.

Séminaire de Québec

Just to the left (north) of the cathedral is the entrance to the **Séminaire de Québec** (Côte de la Fabrique), founded in 1663, and its fabulous **Musée de l'Amérique Francophone** (Museum of French-Speaking America; www.mcq.org/en/informations/maf; 2 Côte de la Fabrique). American officers were imprisoned here after their unsuccessful siege of Québec in 1775–76. Detour down pretty Rue Garneau, then descend to Rue des Remparts for fine views over Québec City's waterfront factory district.

The Walk >> Descend Côte de la Canoterie, a historical link between the Lower and Upper

Towns. Turn right at Rue St-Thomas and then right again onto Rue St-Paul.

Rue St-Paul & Antiques Row

Rue St-Paul is lined with galleries, antiquarian shops and bric-a-brac stores and is always a delightful place to stroll and browse.

The Walk >> Turn right and follow pretty Rue Sault-au-Matelot to the impressive Québec fresco.

Fresque des Québécois

The impressive 420-sq-meter trompe l'oeil **Fresque des Québécois** (Québec City Mural; 29 Rue Notre-Dame, Parc de la Cetière) is where you can pose for the requisite tourist pic alongside historical figures like Jacques Cartier and Samuel de Champlain. The whimsical multistory mural was painted in 1998 by a group of artists from Québec and Lyon in France.

The Walk >> The easiest way to return to Porte St-Louis is to take the funicular up to the Old Upper Town, walk across Place d'Armes to the Château Frontenac and then walk southwest along Rue St-Louis.

9pm Wed year-round) Spare at least a half-day to visit this extraordinary art museum, one of the province's best. Permanent exhibitions range from art in the early French colonies to Québec's contemporary artists, with individual halls devoted entirely to 20th-century artistic giants such as Jean-Paul Lemieux, Fernand Leduc and Jean-Paul Riopelle. Arguably the museum's highlight is the Brousseau Collection of Inuit Art, a selection of 100 pieces by 60 artists located at the top of the Pavillon Pierre Lassonde.

🏃 Activities & Tours

★ Corridor du Littoral & Promenade Samuel-de-Champlain   CYCLING, WALKING

(🌐) 🏄 Starting southwest of Québec City at Cap-Rouge and extending northeast via the Old Lower Town to Montmorency Falls, the Corridor du Littoral is a 48km multipurpose recreation path along the St Lawrence River, popular with cyclists, walkers and in-line skaters. The heart of the path is the Promenade Samuel-de-Champlain, an especially beautiful 2.5km section.

★ Lévis Ferry   BOATING

(🌐 877-787-7483; www.traversiers.com; 10 Rue des Traversiers, Gare Fluviale de Québec, Old Lower Town & Port; car & driver/adult/child one way $8.65/3.65/2.45) For city views, you can't beat the 12-minute ferry ride to Lévis; boats operate from 6am to 2am, departing every 30 to 60 minutes depending on the time, day and season. If you purchase a round-trip ticket, you must disembark for security reasons. There's usually a 20-minute layover in Lévis.

Cyclo Services   CYCLING

(🌐 418-692-4052, 877-692-4050; www.cycloservices. net; 289 Rue St-Paul, Old Lower Town & Port; rental per 2/24hr city bike $17/38, electric bike $34/76; ⊙ 9am-5:30pm Mon-Fri, 10am-5pm Sat & Sun, variable hours Nov-Apr; 🌐) This outfit rents a variety of bikes (city, tandem, road, electric, kids') and organizes excellent cycling tours of the city and outskirts to places such as Wendake (half-day $95) and La Chute Montmorency (four hours $77). The knowledgeable and fun guides frequently give tours in English. In winter it rents snowshoes only ($15), and hours are limited; call ahead.

Les Tours Voir Québec   WALKING

(🌐 418-694-2001, 866-694-2001; www.tours voirquebec.com; 12 Rue Ste-Anne, Old Upper Town; walking tour adult/student/child $23/19.50/11) This group offers excellent tours on the history, architecture and food of Québec City. The popular two-hour 'grand tour,' probably the city's best walking tour, takes in the Old City's highlights, while the food tour includes tastings of wines, cheeses, crepes and chocolate at a variety of shops and restaurants. Buy tickets at and depart from Centre Infotouriste Québec City (p105).

Patinoire de la Place d'Youville   ICE-SKATING

(Place d'Youville Skating Rink; 🌐 418-641-6256; www.quebec-cite.com/en/businesses/outdoor-activities/snow/skating/patinoire-de-la-place-dyouville; 995 Place d'Youville, St-Jean-Baptiste; skating free, skate rental $9.25; ⊙ noon-10pm Mon-Thu, 10am-10pm Fri-Sun mid-Nov–mid-Mar; 🌐) In the shadow of Old Québec's walls, this improvised outdoor rink is one of the most scenic and popular places for ice-skating once winter rolls around. It's a great place to mingle with locals, and you can also rent skates at the nearby Pavillon des Services.

🎊 Festivals & Events

Carnaval de Québec   CARNIVAL

(Québec Winter Carnival; 🌐 866-422-7628, 418-626-3716; www.carnaval.qc.ca; ⊙ Feb) This annual event is unique to Québec City. It bills itself as the world's biggest winter carnival, with parades, ice sculptures, a snow slide, boat races, dances, music and lots of drinking over 17 days. Activities take place all over town and the iconic slide is on the Terrasse Dufferin (p99) behind the Château Frontenac.

🛏 Sleeping

From old-fashioned B&Bs to stylish boutique hotels, Québec City has some fantastic overnight options. The best choices are the numerous small European-style hotels and Victorian B&Bs scattered around the Old Town. However, prices are drastically lower and rooms bigger outside the walls, and for drivers, parking suddenly becomes a less complicated affair.

🛏 Outside the Walls

Centre de Plein Air de Beauport   CAMPGROUND $

(🌐 418-641-6112, 877-641-6113; www.centreplein airbeauport.ca; 95 Rue de la Sérénité, Beauport; campsites & RV sites $38-48; ⊙ Jun-early Sep; P 🐾) This excellent campground near Montmorency Falls is green, peaceful and just a 15-minute drive from Old Québec. To get there, take Hwy 40 toward Montmorency, get off at exit 321 and turn north.

★ Auberge JA Moisan
B&B $$

(☎ 418-529-9764; www.jamoisan.com; 695 Rue St-Jean, St-Jean-Baptiste; s $110-170, d $120-180; P ❄ 🛜) This lovely B&B above the historical JA Moisan grocery store (p105) has four relatively small bedrooms tucked under the eaves and gorgeously furnished in period style. The floor below holds common areas, including a parlor, tearoom, solarium, terrace and computer room. Gregarious host Clément St-Laurent makes guests feel right at home. Rates include breakfast, afternoon tea and valet parking.

Château des Tourelles
B&B $$

(☎ 418-647-9136, 866-346-9136; www.chateaudestourelles.qc.ca; 212 Rue St-Jean, St-Jean-Baptiste; r $99-183, ste $129-245; P ❄ @ 🛜) You'll recognize this B&B by its soaring turret, which mirrors the steeple of the Church of St-Jean-Baptiste to the east. The affable Breton owner has completely refurbished this old house, equipping the 11 rooms with wood floors, triple-paned windows, hi-def TV and new bath; other perks include the bright-orange-hued breakfast area and lounge, and rooftop terrace with great views.

🛏 Inside the Walls

★ Le Monastère des Augustines
HISTORIC HOTEL $$

(☎ 418-694-1639, 844-694-1639; https://monastere.ca/fr/hebergement; 77 Rue des Remparts, Old Upper Town; r $184-230, with shared bath $130-160; P ❄ 🛜) Attached to the convent museum (p99), this fabulous hostelry is the most atmospheric place to stay in Québec City. Choose among 32 'authentic' rooms (shared bath) – former cells inhabited by the nuns when it was a much larger working convent – or 33 'modern' rooms in a new wing with all the usual commodities.

There's an attached restaurant serving multicourse set meals ($24) at 6pm and 7pm Thursday to Saturday. The monastery is a nonprofit organization and all proceeds go to the Augustinian Sisters Heritage Fund.

★ Maison Historique James Thompson
B&B $$

(☎ 418-694-9042; www.bedandbreakfastquebec.com; 47 Rue Ste-Ursule, Old Upper Town; r $75-135; P ❄ 🛜) History buffs will get a real kick out of staying in the 18th-century former residence of James Thompson, a veteran of the Battle of the Plains of Abraham. The beautifully restored house comes complete with the original murder hole next to the front door. The three rooms are spacious – check out the High Priestess.

★ Fairmont Le Château Frontenac
HOTEL $$$

(☎ 866-540-4460, 418-692-3861; www.fairmont.com/frontenac; 1 Rue des Carrières, Old Upper Town; r $229-700, ste $408-2700; P ❄ 🛜 🐾) More than a hotel, the iconic Frontenac is Québec City's most enduring symbol. Its 611 rooms come in a dozen-plus categories. The coveted river-view rooms – beg, borrow or steal room 1001 – range in price from Deluxe units tucked under the 18th-floor eaves to the 60 ultraspacious Fairmont Gold rooms, with concierge service, curved turret windows and vintage architectural details.

★ Auberge St-Antoine
DESIGN HOTEL $$$

(☎ 888-692-2211, 418-692-2211; www.saint-antoine.com; 8 Rue St-Antoine, Old Lower Town & Port; r $259-429, ste $720-1450; P ❄ @ 🛜) Auberge St-Antoine is probably Québec's finest smaller hotel, with phenomenal service and endless amenities. The 95 plush and spacious rooms come with high-end mattresses, goose-down duvets, luxury linens and atmospheric lighting, while the halls resemble an art gallery, filled with French-colonial artifacts from the 18th and 19th centuries uncovered during excavations to expand the hotel.

✗ Eating

Québec City's restaurant scene has never been better. While the capital has always excelled at classic French food, a number of new arrivals have put a trendy modern spin on bistros. Better places can get a bit pricey, but remember: a carefully chosen *table d'hôte* (fixed-price menu) at lunchtime will give you exactly the same food for a more manageable price.

Le Croquembouche
BAKERY $

(☎ 418-523-9009; www.lecroquembouche.com; 225 Rue St-Joseph Est, St-Roch; pastries from $2, sandwiches from $5.25; ⏱ 7am-6:30pm Tue-Sat, to 5pm Sun; 🐾) Widely hailed as Québec City's finest bakery, Le Croquembouche draws devoted locals from dawn to dusk. Among its seductive offerings are fluffy-as-a-cloud croissants, tantalizing cakes and éclairs, brioches brimming with raspberries, and gourmet sandwiches on fresh-baked bread. There's also a stellar array of *danoises* (Danish pastries), including orange and anise, cranberry, pistachio and chocolate.

★ 1608
CHEESE $$

(☎ 418-692-3861; http://1608baravin.com; 1 Rue des Carrières, Fairmount Le Château Frontenac, Old Upper Town; mains $21-34; ⊙ 4pm-midnight Sun-Thu, 2pm-1am Fri & Sat) At this Frontenac-based wine-and-cheese bar you can either select some cheeses yourself or let the staff take you down a wine-and-cheese rabbit hole that's difficult to emerge from; platters of three/four/five cheeses are $21/26/30 (five types with charcuterie $34). Wine, *fromage* and an incomparable view of the St Lawrence all make for a very romantic setting.

★ Le Lapin Sauté
FRENCH $$

(☎ 418-692-5325; www.lapinsaute.com; 52 Rue du Petit-Champlain, Old Lower Town & Port; mains $17-29; ⊙ 11am-10pm Mon-Fri, 9am-10pm Sat & Sun) Naturally, *lapin* (rabbit) plays a starring role at this cozy, rustic restaurant just south of the funicular's lower terminus, in such dishes as rabbit cassoulet or rabbit poutine. Other enticements include salads, French onion soup, charcuterie platters and an excellent-value lunch menu (from $16).

★ Battuto
ITALIAN $$

(☎ 418-614-4414; www.battuto.ca; 527 Blvd Langelier, St-Roch; mains $21-23; ⊙ 5:30-10pm Tue-Sat) Considered by many Québécois to be the best Italian restaurant in town, this wonderful place on the edge of St-Roch mixes traditional dishes like *vitello tonnato* (veal topped with a tuna sauce) with more inventive pasta ones such as Sicilian *casarecce* served with sweetbreads and sherry. It's a tiny place, with a mere 24 seats, so book well ahead.

★ Le St-Amour
FRENCH, QUÉBÉCOIS $$$

(☎ 418-694-0667; www.saint-amour.com; 48 Rue Ste-Ursule, Old Upper Town; mains $42-52, tasting menus $72 & $130; ⊙ 11:30am-2pm Mon-Fri, 5:30-10pm daily) One of Québec City's top-end darlings, Le St-Amour has earned a loyal following for its beautifully prepared grills and seafood, and luxurious surrounds. The soaring greenhouse-style ceiling trimmed with hanging plants creates an inviting setting, and the midday *table d'hôte* ($18 to $33; available weekdays) offers that rarest of Upper Town experiences – a world-class meal at an extremely reasonable price.

🍺 Drinking & Nightlife

★ Le Sacrilège
BAR

(☎ 418-649-1985; www.lesacrilege.com; 447 Rue St-Jean, St-Jean-Baptiste; ⊙ noon-3am) With its unmistakable sign of a laughing, dancing monk saucily lifting his robes, this bar has long been the watering hole of choice for Québec's night owls. Even on Monday, it's standing room only. There's a quite good selection of beers (including many craft varieties), live music most nights at 8pm and seating on a lovely garden terrace out back.

★ Noctem Artisans Brasseurs
MICROBREWERY

(☎ 581-742-7979; www.noctem.ca; 438 Rue du Parvis, St-Roch; ⊙ 11am-3am) One of the most interesting microbreweries in town, Noctem goes beyond the *blonde* (lager), *blanche* (white), *rousse* (red) and IPA tick list to offer a blackboard of up to 18 different beers and ales that change daily. If peckish, eschew the pizza/burger/taco choices in favor of a platter of charcuterie to share.

☆ Entertainment

The performing arts are in fine form in Québec City. Live-performance venues abound, from concert halls to open-air amphitheaters, little jazz and rock clubs, and exuberant *boîtes à chanson* (Québec folk-music clubs), where generations of locals dance and sing with uncensored glee. French-language theater is also an interesting scene, with tons of small companies.

Scanner Bistro
LIVE MUSIC

(☎ 418-523-1916; www.scannerbistro.com; 291 Rue St-Vallier Est, St-Roch; cover charge $5-12; ⊙ 4pm-3am Tue-Fri, 8pm-3am Sat-Mon) Ask any local between the ages of 18 and 35 to suggest a cool place for a drink and this is where they might send you. DJs and live bands serve up a potent musical mix, from heavy metal to hard rock to punk to rockabilly. There's a terrace outside in summer, plus table football and pool inside year-round.

Fou-Bar
LIVE MUSIC

(☎ 418-522-1987; www.foubar.ca; 525 Rue St-Jean, St-Jean-Baptiste; ⊙ 2:30pm-1am Sun & Mon, to 2am Tue & Wed, to 3am Thu-Sat) Laid-back and offering an eclectic mix of bands, this bar is one of the town's classics for good live music. It's also popular for its reasonably priced food menu and its free *pique-assiettes* (literally 'freeloaders' aka appetizers) on Thursday and Friday evenings.

🛍 Shopping

Small, unique and authentic little boutiques are Québec City's claim to retail fame. The best streets for aimless window-shopping

Canoe racing on St Lawrence River during the Carnaval de Québec (p102)

include Rue du Petit-Champlain and Rue St-Paul in the Old Lower Town, Ave Cartier in Montcalm, Rue St-Joseph in St-Roch, and Rue St-Jean (inside and outside the walls).

★ **JA Moisan Épicier** FOOD
(☎418-522-0685; www.jamoisan.com; 695 Rue St-Jean, St-Jean-Baptiste; ☻8:30am-7pm Mon-Wed & Sat, to 9pm Thu & Fri, 10am-7pm Sun, extended hours summer) Established in 1871, this charming store bills itself as North America's oldest grocery. It's a browser's dream come true, packed with beautifully displayed edibles and household items alongside antique cash registers and wood shelving.

You'll find items here you've never seen before, along with heaps of local goods and gift ideas.

Galerie d'Art Inuit Brousseau ART
(☎418-694-1828; www.artinuit.ca; 35 Rue St-Louis, Old Upper Town; ☻9:30am-5:30pm) Devoted to Inuit soapstone, serpentine and basalt carvings and sculptures from artists all over Arctic Canada, this place is gorgeously set up and elaborately lit, with well-trained staff who knowledgeably answer questions. Works range from the small to the large and intricate. Expect high quality and steep prices. International shipping is available.

ⓘ Information

Centre Infotouriste Québec City (Québec Original; ☎877-266-5687, 418-641-6290; www.quebecoriginal.com; 12 Rue Ste-Anne, Old Upper Town; ☻9am-5pm Nov-Jun, to 6pm Jul-Oct) Québec City's main tourist office, in the heart of the Old Town, opposite the Château Frontenac.

ⓘ Getting There & Around

Québec City lies about 260km northeast of Montréal (three hours by car). The most common routes are Autoroute 20, on the south shore of the St Lawrence River, and the slightly longer Autoroute 40 along the north shore. However, compact Old Québec lends itself better to exploration on foot than by car. If you're driving up here, plan to park your vehicle for as much of your stay as possible. Parking garages in and around the Old Town typically charge a day rate of $17.50 to $25 Monday to Friday, and $8 to $12 overnight and on weekends.

AROUND QUÉBEC CITY

Île d'Orléans

Before Jacques Cartier named Île d'Orléans in honor of the Duke of Orleans, it was known as L'Île de Bacchus for its wild grapes. Today, there's no sign of Dionysian debauchery on sleepy Île d'Orléans, 15km northeast of Québec City, but there is plenty to attract visitors. The island (population 6825), still primarily a farming region, has emerged as the epicenter of Québec's agritourism movement. Foodies from all around flock to the local *économusées* (workshops) to watch culinary artisans making everything from cider to nougat. One 60km-long road encircles the island, with two more cutting across it north–south. Their edges are dotted with strawberry fields, orchards, cider producers, windmills, workshops and galleries.

◉ Sights & Activities

La Forge à Pique-Assaut GALLERY
(☑ 418-828-9300; www.forge-pique-assaut.com; 2200 Chemin Royal, St-Laurent; ⊙ 9am-5pm late Jun-early Sep, 9am-noon & 1:30-5pm Mon-Fri mid-Sep–mid-Jun) Artisan blacksmith Guy Bel makes star railings and decorative objects at this *économusée*.

Maison Drouin HISTORIC BUILDING
(☑ 418-829-0330; www.maisondrouin.com; 2958 Chemin Royal, Ste-Famille; adult/child $6/free; ⊙ 10am-6pm mid-Jun–early Sep, noon-4pm Sat & Sun early Sep–mid-Oct) 🕊 This old house was built in 1730 and is one of the most fascinating stops on the island as it was never modernized (ie no electricity or running water) even though it was inhabited as recently as 1984. Guides in period dress give tours of the house in summer.

Québec Aventure Tours CYCLING
(☑ 418-828-2048; https://quebecaventuretours.com; 507 Rte Prévost, St-Laurent; 5hr road bike/electric bike/tandem/scooter $50/60/60/100; ⊙ 9:30am-6pm May-Oct) Hires out traditional bikes in addition to electric bikes, tandems and scooters. It also runs a daily shuttle ($20) departing from here for the Place d'Armes in Québec City at 9am, returning at 5:15pm.

🛏 Sleeping & Eating

Camping Orléans CAMPGROUND $
(☑ 888-829-2953, 418-829-2953; www.camping orleans.com; 3547 Chemin Royal, St-François; campsites $38-65; ⊙ mid-May–mid-Oct; P 🛜 ❄) This leafy site is at the water's edge at the far end of the island from the bridge. It's the only campground left in the greater Québec City area. There's a swimming pool and pub on-site.

★ Auberge La Goéliche BOUTIQUE HOTEL $$
(☑ 888-511-2248, 418-828-2248; www.goeliche.ca; 22 Rue du Quai, Ste-Pétronille; r $198-228; P ❄ 🛜 ❄) Probably the nicest place to stay on the island, the Victorian-style Auberge La Goéliche has 19 rooms individually decorated with antiques and wood furniture; all of them have balconies and stunning views of the river. Guests can relax on the large porch, in the gardens or by the outdoor pool.

The in-house restaurant (mains $23-29; ⊙ noon-2pm & 5:30-9pm May-Oct, dinner Fri & Sat, weekend brunch only winter) is top class.

La Boulange BAKERY $
(☑ 418-829-3162; www.laboulange.ca; 4624 Chemin Royal, St-Jean; light meals $5-12; ⊙ 7:30am-5:30pm Mon-Sat, to 5pm Sun late-Jun–early Sep, see website for times outside these months) A memorable bakery with a small irresistible store, La Boulange is the perfect spot for a light lunch of sandwiches or pizza, or to gather picnic supplies. Devour to-die-for croissants while taking in views of the St Lawrence and the 18th-century Église St-Jean (p47) next door.

Le Moulin de St-Laurent MEDITERRANEAN $$
(☑ 418-829-3888; www.moulinstlaurent.qc.ca; 754 Chemin Royal, St-Laurent; mains $18-28, set menus $37-47; ⊙ 11:30am-2:30pm & 5:30-8:30pm May-Oct) You'd be hard-pressed to find a more agreeable place to dine than the terrace at the back of this early-19th-century flour mill, with tables inches from a waterfall. The well-prepared, diverse menu is continental with regional flourishes, such as trout and veal. Cottages (from $90) also available.

🛍 Shopping

Chocolaterie de l'Île d'Orléans CHOCOLATE
(☑ 418-828-2252, 800-363-2252; www.chocolaterieorleans.com; 8330 Chemin Royal, Ste-Pétronille; ⊙ 9:30am-5pm Mon-Fri, to 6pm Sat & Sun) Using cocoa beans from Belgium, the chocolatiers above this delightful shop in a 200-year-old house churn out tasty concoctions, including almond bark and flavored truffles. The various assortments come in beautifully colored little paper bags. There's a cozy little cafe attached that serves coffee, cakes, lunch and, in summer, ice cream.

Domaine Steinbach FOOD & DRINKS
(☑ 418-828-0000; www.domainesteinbach.com; 2205 Chemin Royal, St-Pierre; ⊙ 10am-7pm May-Oct, to 5pm Nov & Dec, to 4pm Mar & Apr) This store stocks dozens of farm products, including five ciders made using apples from its organic orchard, one with maple syrup. A tasting flight of five ciders is $4. There is a lovely *gîte* (B&B) next door with four rooms ($135) and a terrace overlooking the river (May to October).

ℹ Information

Île d'Orléans Tourist Office (☑ 866-941-9411, 418-828-9411; http://tourisme.iledorleans.com/en; 490 Côte du Pont, St-Pierre; ⊙ 8:30am-6pm early Jun-early Sep, to 4:30pm rest of year)

QUÉBEC ÎLE D'ORLÉANS

It's worth spending $1 on the *Autour de Île d'Orléans* (Around the Île d'Orléans) brochure at the helpful tourist office, which you'll come to after crossing the Pont de l'Île d'Orléans.

Ste-Anne de Beaupré

You may never fully appreciate how deep Québec's Catholic roots go in its larger cities, but here in the provinces that identity is more than evident, and *here*, in Ste-Anne de Beaupré, it's almost overwhelming. Approaching the town along Rte 138, the twin steeples of the 1920s basilica tower above the motels, *dépanneurs* (convenience stores) and souvenir shops. It's one of the few remaining mega-attractions in the province related not to nature or artificial diversions, but to faith. Since the mid-1600s, the village has been an important Christian site; the annual pilgrimage around the feast day of St Anne (July 26) draws thousands of visitors.

CHARLEVOIX

Charlevoix is a stunning outdoor playground. In summer, the brilliant blue sky is matched by the deep azure of the St Lawrence, while the hills, lined with hiking trails, are carpeted in green. Fall brings colorful foliage, and in winter, snowcapped mountains loom above the rural valleys. For 200 years, this pastoral skein of streams and rolling hills has been a summer retreat for the wealthy and privileged. Unesco classified the entire area a World Biosphere Reserve, which resulted in worthwhile restrictions on the types of permitted developments, and a sense of pride among residents. There's also a lot to be proud of in the lovely towns such as Baie St Paul, with *ateliers* (artists' studios), galleries and boutiques lining its narrow streets.

Baie St Paul

Of all the little towns that lie within day-tripping distance of Québec City, this beautiful blend of the outdoors and the bohemian – this is Cirque du Soleil's hometown – may be the most attractive. Not that we recommend day-tripping: if you're coming to Baie St Paul, book a night in a historic house converted into a superb *gîte*, linger over local cuisine, have a glass of wine and set your watch to the estuarine rhythm of the St Lawrence and Gouffre Rivers.

POUTINE, BIEN SÛR

Like all fast food, Québec's beloved poutine is perfect if you have a *gueule de bois* (hangover) after a night on the Boréale Blonde. In the calorie-packing culinary Frankenstein, the province's exemplary fries (fresh-cut, never frozen or served limp and greasy) are sprinkled with cheese curds and smothered in gravy. The dish was devised in the early 1980s and spread across Québec like a grease fire. Poutine is a staple of roadside diners, *cantines* or *casse croûtes*, where you can sample embellished versions such as Italienne – with spaghetti. Some eateries have their own top-secret recipe; for example, Le Mouton Noir (☑819-322-1571; www.bistromoutonnoir. com; 2301 Rue de l'Église; mains $7.50-14.50; ☺8am-10:30pm Mon-Thu, to 1am Fri, 10am-10:30pm Sat & Sun, closed Mon & Tue winter) in Val-David has a version with guacamole, tomatoes and sour cream. Other great spots include Poutineville (☑581-981-8188; www.poutineville.com; 735 Rue St-Joseph Est, St-Roch; mains $12-16; ☺11am-10pm Sun-Wed, to 11pm Thu, to midnight Fri & Sat) in Québec City and renowned La Banquise (p92) in Montréal.

◉ Sights & Activities

Parc National des Grands Jardins PARK
(☑418-439-1227; www.sepaq.com/pq/grj; adult/child $8.75/free; ◉) Excellent hiking and rugged topography are the lures at this provincial park, which covers 310 sq km, much of it taiga. The hills frame more than 100 small lakes, and if you're lucky, you might spot caribou. The 8.6km (round-trip) trek up Mont du Lac-des-Cygnes (Swan Lake Mountain) is an exceptional half-day hike. You can test your climbing prowess on the Via Ferrata (adult/youth from $48.50/36.25, June to mid-October), with two guided climbing routes.

Musée d'Art Contemporain de Baie St Paul MUSEUM
(☑418-435-3681; www.macbsp.com; 23 Rue Ambroise-Fafard; adult/student/child $10/7/free; ◉10am-5pm mid-Jun–Aug, 11am-5pm Tue-Sun Sep–mid-Jun) This attention-grabbing gallery houses contemporary art by local artists and some photographic exhibits both from its own 3000-piece collection or on loan from the National Gallery of Canada.

Katabatik
KAYAKING

(☑ 800-453-4850; www.katabatik.ca; 210 Rue Ste-Anne; half-day sea-kayaking tours adult/youth $64/49, half-day canyoning adult/youth $94/74, paragliding $114; ⊙ 8am-6:30pm Jul & Aug, 9am-4:30pm Sun-Fri, to 6pm Sat May & Jun, 9am-4pm Tue-Sun Sep & early Oct; 🚲) 🛈 One of the most well-established outdoor/adventure tour companies in Charlevoix, Katabatik offers, among other services, sea-kayaking tours, canyoning and tandem paragliding.

🛏 Sleeping & Eating

Gite Fleury
B&B $

(☑ 418-435-3668; http://gitefleury.com; 102 Rue St-Joseph; r from $83; P ✳ ☎) François and Mario, the proprietors of this cute-as-a-kitten B&B, are simultaneously classy and hospitable, and cook up a mean breakfast to boot. They're happy to offer advice to those who want to tromp through the seaside villages and alpine highlands of Charlevoix, but you may be tempted to crash out in one of their four cozy, simply appointed bedrooms.

Auberge à l'Ancrage
INN $$

(☑ 666-344-3264, 418-240-3264; www.aubergeancrage.com; 29 Rue Ste-Anne; r from $169) Arguably the most charming place to stay in Baie St Paul, this little inn on the Rivière du Gouffre counts but four rooms – two facing the river and two the street. There's a kind of maritime theme going on at the 'Anchorage,' with lots of antiques in public areas and a wonderful porch.

★ Le Diapason
ALSATIAN $$

(☑ 418-435-2929; www.restolediapason.com; 1 Rue Ste-Anne; mains $19-32; ⊙ 11:30am-2pm & 5-9pm) This pleasant surprise (Alsatian in Charlevoix?) serves all our favorites from eastern France: *flammekueche* (Alsatian 'pizza'), *tartiflette* (potatoes roasted with cheese) and, of course, *choucroute garnie* (sauerkraut simmered with assorted smoked meats and sausages). All the produce is locally sourced, the atmosphere more than convivial and the terrace a delight in summer.

Le Mouton Noir
FRENCH $$$

(☑ 418-240-3030; www.moutonnoirresto.com; 43 Rue Ste-Anne; set meals $37-43; ⊙ 11am-3pm & 5-11pm, evenings only Wed-Sun winter) Since 1978 the rustic-looking 'Black Sheep' has been home to fine French cuisine. Fish – including walleye, the freshwater queen – is on offer when available, as are buffalo, caribou and steak, all enlivened by a deft touch that

incorporates wild mushrooms and local produce. The outdoor terrace overlooks the Rivière du Gouffre. Reservations advised.

🛈 Information

Baie St Paul Tourist Office (☑ 418-665-4454; www.tourisme-charlevoix.com; 6 Rue St-Jean-Baptiste; ⊙ 9am-6pm May-Sep, to 4pm Oct-Apr)

Charlevoix Tourist Office (☑ 418-665-4454; www.tourisme-charlevoix.com; 444 Blvd Monseigneur de Laval; ⊙ 8:30am-7pm late Jun-Aug, 9am-4pm Sep-late Jun) South of town.

Mont du Lac-des-Cygnes Visitors Center (☑ 418-439-1227; www.sepaq.com/pq/grj; Rte 381, Km 21; ⊙ 8:30am-8pm Sun-Thu, to 9pm Fri & Sat late Jun-late Aug, varies by season Apr-late Jun & late Aug-Dec) Provides information and visitor services for those going to Parc National des Grands Jardins.

La Malbaie

Encompassing six previously separate villages, La Malbaie was one of Canada's early holiday resorts. From the late 19th century, steamers run by the Richelieu and Ontario Navigation Company and Canada Steamship Lines docked here.

Arriving from the south on Rte 362 or the west on Rte 138, the first village is Pointe-au-Pic. This was a holiday destination for the wealthy at the beginning of the 20th century, drawing the elite from as far away as New York. One of its famous residents was former US president William Howard Taft, who had a summer home built here. Ste-Agnès lies to the northwest, away from the St Lawrence. Adjoining Pointe-au-Pic (and technically merged with it) is La Malbaie, which begins west of the Malbaie River and continues to the other side. North of La Malbaie is Rivière Malbaie, while St-Fidèle and the ridiculously cute Cap à l'Aigle are east on Rte 138.

◉ Sights

Les Jardins du Cap à l'Aigle
GARDENS

(☑ 418-665-3747; 625 Rue St-Raphael, Cap à l'Aigle; adult/child $6/free; ⊙ 9am-5pm Jun-Oct) In Cap à l'Aigle, a little village 2km east of La Malbaie, are these gardens, where 800 types of lilac range up the hill between a waterfall, a footbridge and artists selling their daubs. When in full bloom it's a heavenly spot.

Musée de Charlevoix
MUSEUM

(☑ 418-665-4411; www.museedecharlevoix.qc.ca; 10 Chemin du Havre, Pointe-au-Pic; adult/child $8/6; ⊙ 9am-5pm Jun–mid-Oct, 10am-5pm Mon-Fri, 1-5pm

Sat & Sun mid-Oct–May; 🚼) 🖊 One of the most charming provincial museums in Québec, this waterfront gallery portrays the life and times of Charlevoix through a variety of media: from the impact of the meteors that created the valleys making up the town to the lives of log drivers on the river and the role of folk art in this creative region.

Observatoire de l'Astroblème de Charlevoix
OBSERVATORY

(📋 418-324-4522; www.astroblemecharlevoix.org; 595 Côte Bellevue, Pointe-au-Pic; 1/2/3 activities adult $14/26/36, child $7/13/18; ⊙10am-5pm late Jun-early Sep, to 9pm when cloudy; 🚼) Quite an unusual attraction for adults and kids alike is this observatory, which, through multimedia exhibits, looks at how meteors created the valleys on which Charlevoix sits. Another activity involves stargazing, weather permitting (three hours; available by reservation only in May, June, September and October). A third activity is a geological excursion in the area (three hours).

Maison du Bootlegger
HISTORIC BUILDING

(📋 418-439-3711; www.maisondubootlegger.com; 110 Rang du Ruisseau-des-Frênes, Ste-Agnès; adult/child $10/5, meal, tour & entertainment from $45; ⊙10am-4:30pm & 6-11:30pm Jul–mid-Oct, Sat & Sun only Jun & late Oct) This unexpected venue in a conventional-looking 19th-century farmhouse was surreptitiously modified by an American bootlegger during the Prohibition period of the 1920s. Tours reveal the marvel of secret doorways and hidden chambers intended to deter the morality squad. From 6pm, it turns into a party restaurant where meat feasts are accompanied by Al Capone beer in boot-shaped glasses.

🛏 Sleeping & Eating

Camping des Chutes Fraser
CAMPGROUND $

(📋 418-665-2151; www.campingchutesfraser.com; 500 Chemin de la Vallée, La Malbaie; tent & RV sites from $33, cottages from $115; ⊙camping May-Oct, cottages year-round; 🌊) This campground with a waterfall, toward Mont Grand-Fonds park, is idyllic. There's a snack bar, grocery store and laundry on-site, as well as a swimming pool and mini-golf.

Auberge des 3 Canards
INN $$

(📋 800-665-3761, 418-665-3761; www. auberge3canards.com; 115 Côte Bellevue, Pointe-au-Pic; r $145-225, ste $265; P❄🛜🌊) A sprawl-ing white clapboard property looking out to what people call *la mer* (the sea), the 3 Ducks has 48 rooms sporting flat-screen TVs, vintage photos of steamers, local art and balconies overlooking the tennis court (with the St Lawrence behind). The staff are attentive and the restaurant (mains $34 to $42, set dinner $42) features impeccably presented regional cuisine.

Fairmont Le Manoir Richelieu
HISTORIC HOTEL $$$

(📋 866-540-4464, 418-665-3703; www.fairmont. com/richelieu-charlevoix; 181 Rue Richelieu, Pointe-au-Pic; r $199-399, ste from $550; P❄🛜🌊) The gray-stone country cousin of Québec City's Fairmont Le Château Frontenac (p103), this palatial structure with 405 rooms can claim almost as much history and prestige: it dates back to 1899 and was the venue of the 44th G7 summit in 2018. The sprawling, copper-roofed, castle-like structure, rebuilt after a 1927 fire, has two pools, a massive spa and five restaurants.

Pains d'Exclamation
BAKERY $

(📋 418-665-4000; www.painsdexclamation.com; 398 Rue St-Étienne, La Malbaie; sandwiches $7-12; ⊙6:30am-5:30pm, closed Sun & Mon winter) This bakery makes a good lunchtime stop, mainly for the grilled sandwich with a Brie-like local cheese called Le Fleurmier, apples and walnuts. Soups ($6.75) are usually good, too.

Chez Truchon
BISTRO $$$

(📋 418-665-4622, 888-662-4622; www. aubergecheztruchon.com; 1065 Rue Richelieu, Pointe-au-Pic; mains $26-36; ⊙7:30-11:30am Mon-Sat, to 12:30pm Sun, 5:30-8:30pm Mon-Thu, to 9pm Fri-Sun) Considered by some to be the best restaurant in La Malbaie, this bistro-cum-auberge serves Québécois specialties made from local produce at breakfast and dinner only. The double-roomed dining room with hardwood floors and an old fireplace is lovely; views include the St Lawrence and the open kitchen, through a wall of wine bottles.

ℹ Information

Charlevoix Regional Tourist Office (📋 418-665-4454, 800-667-2276; www.tourisme-charlevoix.com; 495 Blvd de Comporté, La Malbaie; ⊙9am-5pm May-late Jun, 8:30am-7pm late Jun–mid-Oct, 9am-5pm mid-Oct–Apr) Located in the center of La Malbaie and serves as the regional tourism office for all of Charlevoix.

ROAD TRIP ESSENTIALS

Canada Driving Guide

Canada is a fabulous place for road trips, with an extensive network of highways, breathtaking scenery and friendly locals to help out if you should lose your way.

DRIVER'S LICENSE & DOCUMENTS

In most provinces, visitors can legally drive for up to three months with their home driver's license. In some, such as British Columbia, this is extended to six months.

If you're spending considerable time in Canada, think about getting an International Driving Permit (IDP), which is valid for one year. Your automobile association at home can issue one for a small fee. Always carry your home license together with the IDP.

INSURANCE

Canadian law requires liability insurance for all vehicles, to cover you for damage caused to property and people.

➡ The minimum requirement is $200,000 in all provinces except Québec, where it is $50,000.

➡ Americans traveling to Canada in their own car should ask their insurance company for a Nonresident Interprovince Motor Vehicle Liability Insurance Card (commonly known as a 'yellow card'), which is accepted as evidence of financial responsibility anywhere in Canada. Although not mandatory, it may come in handy in an accident.

➡ Car-rental agencies offer liability insurance. Collision Damage Waivers (CDW) reduce or eliminate the amount you'll have to reimburse the rental company if there's damage to the car itself. Some credit cards cover CDW for a certain rental period if you use the card to pay for

the rental and decline the policy offered by the rental company. Always check with your card issuer to see what coverage it offers in Canada.

➡ Personal accident insurance (PAI) covers you and any passengers for medical costs incurred as a result of an accident. If your travel insurance or your health-insurance policy at home does this as well (and most do, but check), then this is one expense you can do without.

RENTAL

Car

To rent a car in Canada you generally need to be at least 25 years old (some companies will rent to drivers between the ages of 21 and 24 for an additional charge); hold a valid driver's license (an international one may be required if you're not from an English- or French-speaking country); and have a major credit card.

> ### Driving Fast Facts
>
> **Right or left?** Drive on the right
>
> **Legal driving age** 16
>
> **Top speed limit** Varies by province; 90km/h in Prince Edward Island, 100km/h in Ontario and Québec, and 120km/h in BC
>
> **Best radio station** The ad-free Canadian Broadcasting Corporation (CBC)

111

Canada Playlist

Feist Mushaboom

Wheat Kings The Tragically Hip

Keep the Car Running Arcade Fire

Prémonition Coeur de Pirate

Electric Pow Wow Drum The Halluci Nation

Bridge to Nowhere Sam Roberts

Tôt ou Tard Eli Rose

I Don't Know The Sheepdogs

Colossus of Rhodes The New Pornographers

Crabbuckit K-OS

Fous n'Importe Où Charlotte Cardin & CRi

Heart of Gold Neil Young

When the Night Feels My Song Bedouin Soundclash

Renta-car rates generally include unlimited mileage, but expect surcharges for additional drivers and one-way rentals. Major international car-rental companies usually have branches at airports, train stations and in city centers. In Canada, on-the-spot rentals often are more expensive than pre-booked packages (ie cars booked with a flight or in advance).

Child and infant safety seats are legally required; reserve them (around $15 per day, or $50 per trip) when booking your car.

International car-rental companies with hundreds of branches nationwide include:

Avis (☎800-230-4898; www.avis.com)

Budget (☎800-268-8900, French 800-268-8970; www.budget.com)

Dollar (☎800-800-5252; www.dollar canada.ca)

Enterprise (☎844-307-8008; www.enterprise.ca)

Hertz (☎800-654-3131; www.hertz.com)

National (☎toll free 844-307-8014; www.nationalcar.ca)

Practicar (☎toll free 800-327-0116; www.practicar.ca) Often has lower rates. It's also affiliated with Backpackers Hostels Canada and Hostelling International.

Thrifty (☎800-334-1705; www.thrifty canada.ca)

Motorcycle

Several companies offer motorcycle rentals and tours. A Harley Heritage Softail Classic costs about $210 per day, including liability insurance and 200km mileage. Some companies have minimum rental periods, which can be as much as seven days.

RVs & Campervans

The RV market is biggest in the west, with specialized agencies in Calgary, Edmonton, Whitehorse and Vancouver. For summer travel, book as early as possible. The base cost is roughly $250 per day in high season for smaller vehicles, although insurance, fees and taxes add a hefty chunk to that. Diesel-fueled RVs have considerably lower running costs.

Canadream Campers (☎925-255-8383; www.canadream.com) Based in Calgary, with rentals (including one-way rentals) in eight cit-

Driving Tips

➡ Never let the gas tank go below a third of a tank, even if you think there's cheaper fuel up the road. When traveling out west, always fill up before heading to your next destination. Sometimes, the next station is a long way off!

➡ In some areas you can drive for hours without cell service, so plan carefully for emergencies.

➡ Moose, deer and elk are common on rural roadways, especially at night. There's no contest between a 534kg bull moose and a Subaru, so keep your eyes peeled.

➡ A word for Canada's southern neighbors: don't forget that speed limits are in kilometers - not miles - per hour!

ies, including Vancouver, Whitehorse, Toronto and Halifax.

Cruise Canada (☎403-291-4963; www.cruisecanada.com) Offers three sizes of RVs. Locations in Halifax, and in central and western Canada; offers one-way rentals.

BRINGING YOUR OWN VEHICLE

There's minimal hassle driving into Canada from the USA, as long as you have your vehicle's registration papers, proof of liability insurance and your home driver's license.

MAPS & APPS

➡ **National Geographic Road Atlas** is one of the best ink-and-paper maps, with special attention paid to national parks and forests.

➡ **Google Maps** (http://maps.google.com) offers turn-by-turn driving directions with estimated traffic delays. Be sure to download offline maps so you have mapping details when you lack cell-phone service.

➡ **Waze** (www.waze.com) is a popular, free crowd-sourced traffic and navigation app.

➡ **GasBuddy** (www.gasbuddy.com) is a website and app that finds the cheapest places to gas up nearby.

➡ Most tourist offices distribute free provincial road maps.

➡ You can also download and print maps from **GeoBase** (http://geogratis.gc.ca).

ROAD CONDITIONS

Road conditions are generally good, but there are a few things to keep in mind.

Fierce winters can leave potholes the size of landmine craters. Be prepared to swerve. Winter travel in general can be hazardous due to heavy snow and ice, which may cause roads and bridges to close periodically. **Transport Canada** (☎613-990-2309; www.tc.gc.ca/en/transport-canada.html) provides links to road conditions and construction zones for each province.

If you're driving in winter or in remote areas, make sure your vehicle is equipped with four-season radial or snow tires, and emergency supplies in case you're stranded.

Road Trip Websites

Canadian Automobile Association (www.caa.ca) Offers services, including 24-hour emergency roadside assistance, to members of international affiliates, such as AAA in the USA, AA in the UK and ADAC in Germany. The club also offers trip-planning advice, free maps, travel-agency services and discounts on hotels, car rentals etc. Autoclub membership is a handy thing to have in Canada

Canada Road Conditions (https://www.th.gov.bc.ca/drivebc_supp/canada_map.htm) Check the status of road conditions in all 13 provinces and territories.

ROAD RULES

➡ Canadians drive on the right-hand side of the road.

➡ Seat belt use is compulsory. Children who weigh less than 18kg must be strapped into child-booster seats, except infants, who must be in a rear-facing safety seat.

➡ Motorcyclists must wear helmets and drive with their headlights on.

➡ Distances and speed limits are posted in kilometers. The speed limit is generally 40km/h to 50km/h in cities and 90km/h to 110km/h outside town.

➡ Slow down to 60km/h when passing emergency vehicles (such as police cars and ambulances) stopped on the roadside with their lights flashing.

➡ Turning right at red lights after coming to a full stop is permitted in all provinces (except where road signs prohibit it, and on the island of Montréal, where it's always a no-no). There's a national propensity for running red lights, however, so don't assume 'right of way' at intersections.

➡ Driving while using a hand-held cell phone is illegal in Canada. Fines are hefty.

➡ Radar detectors are not allowed in most of Canada (Alberta, British Columbia and Saskatchewan are the exceptions). If you're caught driving with a radar detector, even one that isn't being operated, you could receive a fine of $1000 and your device may be confiscated.

➡ The blood-alcohol limit for drivers is 0.08%, but provincial limits can be lower. Driving while drunk or high is a criminal offense.

PARKING

Free parking is plentiful in small towns and rural areas, but scarce and often expensive in cities. Municipal parking meters and centralized pay stations usually accept coins and credit or debit cards.

When parking on the street, carefully read all posted regulations and restrictions (eg 30-minute maximum, no parking during scheduled street-cleaning hours) and pay attention to colored curbs, or you may be ticketed and towed. In some towns and cities, overnight street parking is prohibited downtown and in designated areas reserved for local residents with permits.

At city parking garages and lots, expect to pay at least $2 per hour and $12 to $40 for all-day or overnight parking.

FUEL

Most gas stations in Canada are self-service. You'll find them on highways outside of most towns, though the options are few and far between in sparsely populated areas. Gas is sold in liters (3.78L equals one US gallon). The current cost for regular fuel in Canada ranges from $1.10 to $1.55. Prices are higher in remote areas, with Yellowknife usually setting the national record; drivers in Calgary typically pay the least for gas. Fuel prices are usually lower in the USA, so fill up south of the border if that's an option.

SAFETY

Vehicle theft, break-ins and vandalism are a problem mostly in urban areas. Be sure to lock your vehicle's doors, leave the windows rolled up and use any anti-theft devices that have been installed (eg car alarm, steering-wheel lock). Do not leave any valuables visible inside your vehicle; instead, stow them in the trunk before arriving at your destination, or else take them with you once you've parked.

Driving Problem-Buster

What should I do if my car breaks down? Put on your hazard lights (flashers) and carefully pull over to the side of the road. Call the roadside emergency assistance number of your car-rental company or, if you're driving your own car, your automobile association.

What if I have an accident? If it's safe to do so, pull over to the side of the road. For minor collisions with no major property damage or bodily injuries, be sure to exchange driver's license and auto-insurance information with the other driver, then file a report with your insurance provider or notify your car-rental company as soon as possible. If you distrust the other party, call the police, who will fill out an objective report. For major accidents, call 📞911 and wait for the police and emergency services to arrive.

What should I do if I am stopped by the police? Be courteous. Don't get out of the car unless asked. Keep your hands where the officer can see them (eg on the steering wheel). For traffic violations, there is usually a 30-day period to pay a fine; most matters can be handled by mail. Police can legally give roadside sobriety checks to assess if you've been drinking or using drugs.

What should I do if my car gets towed? Immediately call the local police in the town or city that you're in and ask where to pick up your car. Towing and hourly or daily storage fees can quickly total hundreds of dollars.

What if I can't find anywhere to stay? If you're stuck and it's getting late, it's best not to keep driving on aimlessly – just pull into the next roadside chain motel or hotel with the 'Vacancy' light lit up.

Canada Travel Guide

GETTING THERE & AWAY

AIR

Airports & Airlines

Toronto is far and away Canada's busiest airport, followed by Vancouver. The international gateways you're most likely to use:

Calgary (Calgary International Airport; www.yyc.com)

Edmonton (Edmonton International Airport; http://flyeia.com)

Halifax (Halifax Stanfield International Airport; http://halifaxstanfield.ca)

Montréal (Montréal Trudeau International Airport; www.admtl.com)

Ottawa (Ottawa International Airport; http://yow.ca)

St John's (St John's International Airport; http://stjohnsairport.com)

Toronto (Toronto Pearson International Airport; www.torontopearson.com)

Vancouver (Vancouver International Airport; www.yvr.ca)

Winnipeg (Winnipeg International Airport; www.waa.ca)

Air Canada (www.aircanada.com), the national flagship carrier, is considered one of the world's safest airlines. All major global airlines fly to Canada. Other companies based in the country and serving international destinations:

WestJet (www.westjet.com) Calgary-based low-cost carrier serving destinations throughout Canada as well as across the US and Caribbean.

Porter Airlines (www.flyporter.com) Flies around eastern Canada and to US cities,

including Boston, Chicago, Washington, DC, and New York.

Air Transat (www.airtransat.com) Charter airline from major Canadian cities to holiday destinations (ie southern USA and Caribbean in winter, Europe in summer).

CAR & MOTORCYCLE

The highway system of the continental USA connects directly with the Canadian highway system at numerous points along the border. These Canadian highways then meet up with the east–west Trans-Canada Hwy further north. Between the Yukon Territory and Alaska, the main routes are the Alaska, Klondike and Haines Hwys.

If you're driving into Canada, you'll need the vehicle's registration papers, proof of liability insurance and your home driver's license. Cars rented in the USA can usually be driven into Canada and back, but make sure your rental agreement says so. If you're driving a car registered in someone else's name, bring a letter from the owner authorizing use of the vehicle in Canada.

SEA

Ferry

Various ferry services on the coasts connect the USA and Canada:

➡ Bar Harbor, Maine, to Yarmouth, NS: **Bay Ferries Limited** (www.ferries.ca/thecat)

➡ Eastport, Maine, to Deer Island, NB: **East Coast Ferries** (www.eastcoastferriesltd.com)

➡ Seattle, WA, to Victoria, BC: **Victoria Clipper** (www.clippervacations.com)

➡ Ketchikan, Alaska, to Prince Rupert, BC: **Alaska Marine Highway System** (www.ferryalaska.com)

→ Bella Bella, BC, to Prince Rupert, BC: **BC Ferries** (www.bcferries.com)

→ Sandusky, Ohio, to Pelee Island, ON: **Pelee Island Transportation Service** (www.ontarioferries.com)

→ Port Angeles, WA, to Victoria, BC; **Black Ball Ferry** (www.cohoferry.com)

→ Anacortes, WA, to Sidney, BC; **Washington State Ferries** (www.wsdot.wa.gov/ferries)

Freighters

An adventurous, though not necessarily inexpensive, way to travel to or from Canada is aboard a cargo ship. Freighters carry between three and 12 passengers and, though considerably less luxurious than cruise ships, they give a salty taste of life at sea. **Maris Freighter Cruises** (www.freightercruises.com) has more information on the ever-changing routes.

TRAIN

Amtrak (www.amtrak.com) and **VIA Rail Canada** (www.viarail.ca) run three routes between the USA and Canada: two in the east and one in the west. Customs inspections happen at the border, not upon boarding.

Train Routes & Fares

Route	Duration (hr)	Frequency (daily)	Fare (US$)
New York–Toronto (Maple Leaf)	13¾	1	131
New York–Montréal (Adirondack)	12	1	70
Seattle–Vancouver (Cascades)	4	2	41

DIRECTORY A–Z

ACCESSIBLE TRAVEL

Canada is making progress when it comes to easing the everyday challenges facing people with disabilities, especially those who have mobility requirements.

→ Many public buildings, including museums, tourist offices, train stations, shopping malls and cinemas, have access ramps and/or lifts. Most public restrooms feature extra-wide stalls equipped with hand rails. Many pedestrian crossings have sloping curbs.

→ Newer and recently remodeled hotels, especially chain hotels, have rooms with extra-wide doors and spacious bathrooms.

→ Interpretive centers at national and provincial parks are usually accessible, and many parks have trails that can be navigated in wheelchairs.

→ Car-rental agencies offer hand-controlled vehicles and vans with wheelchair lifts at no additional charge, but you must reserve them well in advance.

→ Download Lonely Planet's free Accessible Travel guides from http://lptravel.to/AccessibleTravel.

→ For accessible air, bus, rail and ferry transportation, check **Access to Travel** (www.accesstotravel.gc.ca), the federal government's website. In general, most transportation agencies can accommodate people with disabilities if you make your needs known when booking.

Other organizations specializing in the needs of travelers with disabilities:

Mobility International (www.miusa.org) Advises travelers with disabilities on mobility issues and runs an educational exchange program.

Society for Accessible Travel & Hospitality (www.sath.org) Travelers with disabilities share tips and blogs.

ACCOMMODATIONS

In popular destinations, such as Ottawa, Banff and Jasper, it pays to book ahead in the height of the summer, especially during major festivals, and in the ski season.

B&Bs From purpose-built villas to heritage homes or someone's spare room, they are often the most atmospheric lodgings.

Motels Dotting the highways into town, these are often family-run affairs that offer the most bang for your buck.

Hotels From standard to luxurious with a burgeoning number of boutique options.

Hostels Young backpacker hangouts, but favored by outdoor adventurers in remoter regions.

Camping Campgrounds are plentiful; private grounds often have fancier facilities.

Seasons

➡ Peak season is summer, basically June through August, when prices are highest.

➡ It's best to book ahead during summer, as well as during ski season at winter resorts, and during holidays and major events, as rooms can be scarce.

➡ Some properties close down altogether in the off-season.

B&Bs

➡ **Bed & Breakfast Online** (http://m.bbcanada.com) is the main booking agency for properties nationwide.

➡ In Canada, B&Bs (*gîtes* in French) are essentially converted or purpose-built private homes whose owners live on-site. People who like privacy may find B&Bs too intimate, as walls are rarely soundproof and it's usual to mingle with your hosts and other guests.

➡ Standards vary widely, sometimes even within a single B&B. The cheapest rooms tend to be small, with few amenities and a shared bathroom. Nicer ones have added features such as a balcony, a fireplace and an en suite bathroom.

➡ Breakfast is always included in the rates (though it might be continental instead of a full cooked affair).

➡ Not all B&Bs accept children.

➡ Minimum stays (usually two nights) are common, and many B&Bs are only open seasonally.

Hotels & Motels

Most hotels are part of international chains, and the newer ones are designed for either the luxury market or businesspeople, with in-room cable TV and wi-fi. Many also have swimming pools and fitness and business centers. Rooms with two double or queen-sized beds sleep up to four people, although there is usually a small surcharge for the third and fourth people. Many places advertise 'kids stay free,' but sometimes you have to pay extra for a crib or a rollaway (portable bed).

In Canada, like the USA (both lands of the automobile), motels are ubiquitous. They dot the highways and cluster in groups on the outskirts of towns and cities. Although most motel rooms won't win any style awards, they're usually clean and comfortable and offer good value for travelers. Many regional motels remain typical mom-and-pop operations, but plenty of North American chains have also opened up across the country.

Camping

➡ Canada is filled with campgrounds – some federal or provincial, others privately owned.

➡ The official season runs from May to September, but exact dates vary by location.

➡ Facilities vary widely. Backcountry sites offer little more than pit toilets and fire rings, and have no potable water. Unserviced (tent) campgrounds come with access to drinking water and a washroom with toilets and

Practicalities

Newspapers The most widely available newspaper is the Toronto-based *Globe and Mail*. Other principal dailies are the *Montréal Gazette, Ottawa Citizen, Toronto Star* and *Vancouver Sun*. *Maclean's* is Canada's weekly news magazine.

Radio & TV The Canadian Broadcasting Corporation (CBC) is the dominant nationwide network for both radio and TV. The CTV Television Network is its major competition.

Smoking Banned in all restaurants, bars and other public venues nationwide. This includes tobacco, vaping and cannabis.

Weights & Measures Canada officially uses the metric system, but imperial measurements are used for many day-to-day purposes.

sometimes showers. The best-equipped sites feature flush toilets and hot showers, and water, electrical and sewer hookups for recreational vehicles (RVs).

➡ Private campgrounds sometimes cater only to trailers (caravans) and RVs, and may feature convenience stores, playgrounds and swimming pools. It is a good idea to phone ahead to make sure the size of sites and the services provided at a particular campground are suitable for your vehicle.

➡ Most government-run sites are available on a first-come, first-served basis and fill up quickly, especially in July and August. Several national parks participate in Parks Canada's **camping reservation program** (☑519-826-5391; http://reservation.pc.gc.ca; reservation fee online/call center $11/13.50), which is a convenient way to make sure you get a spot.

➡ Nightly camping fees in national and provincial parks range from $25 to $35 (a bit more for full-hookup sites); fire permits often cost a few dollars extra. Backcountry camping costs about $10 per night. Private campgrounds tend to be a bit pricier. British Columbia's parks, in particular, have seen a hefty rate increase in recent years.

➡ Some campgrounds remain open for maintenance year-round and may let you camp at a reduced rate in the off-season. This can be great in late autumn or early spring, when there's hardly a soul about. Winter camping, though, is only for the hardy.

DISCOUNT CARDS

Discounts are commonly offered for seniors, children, families and people with disabilities, though no special cards are issued (you get the savings on-site when you pay). AAA and other automobile association members can also receive various travel-related discounts.

International Student Identity Card (www.isic.org) Provides students with discounts on travel insurance and admission to museums and other sights. There are also cards for those who are under 26 years but not students, and for full-time teachers.

Parks Canada Discovery Pass (adult/family $68/137; www.pc.gc.ca) Provides access to more than 100 national parks and historic sites for a year. Can pay for itself in as few as seven visits; also provides quicker entry into sites. Note that there's no charge for kids under 18 years, and a 'family' can include up to seven people in a vehicle, even if they're unrelated.

Many cities have discount cards for local attractions, such as the following:

Montréal Museum Pass (www.musees montreal.org; $75)

Ottawa Museums Passport (www. museumspassport.ca; $35)

Toronto CityPASS (www.citypass.com/toronto; adult/child $73/50)

Vanier Park ExplorePass (Vancouver; www.spacecentre.ca/explore-pass; adult/child $42.50/36.50)

ELECTRICITY

Type A
120V/60Hz

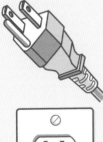

Type B
120V/60Hz

FOOD

Canadian cuisine is nothing if not eclectic, a casserole of food cultures blended together from centuries of immigration. Poutine (French fries topped with gravy and cheese curds), Montréal-style bagels, salmon jerky and pierogi jostle for comfort-food attention. For something more refined,

Montréal, Toronto and Vancouver have well-seasoned fine-dining scenes, while regions across the country have rediscovered the unique ingredients grown, foraged and produced on their doorsteps – bringing distinctive seafood, artisan cheeses and lip-smacking produce to menus.

It's worth booking ahead for popular places, especially on the weekend – which, in the Canadian restaurant world, includes Thursdays. Most cafes and budget restaurants don't accept reservations.

Local Flavors

Starting from the east, the main dish of the Maritime provinces is lobster – boiled in the pot and served with a little butter – and the best place to sample it is a community hall 'kitchen party' on Prince Edward Island. Dip into some chunky potato salad and hearty seafood chowder while waiting for your crustacean to arrive, but don't eat too much; you'll need room for the mountainous fruit pie coming your way afterward.

Next door, Nova Scotia visitors should save their appetites for butter-soft Digby scallops and rustic Lunenburg sausage, while the favored meals of nearby Newfoundland and Labrador often combine rib-sticking dishes of cod cheeks and sweet snow crab. If you're feeling really ravenous, gnaw on a slice of seal-flipper pie – a dish you're unlikely to forget in a hurry.

Québec is the world's largest maple-syrup producer, processing an annual 60 million liters (13.2 million gallons) of the syrup used on pancakes and in myriad other dishes. In this French-influenced province, fine food is a lifeblood for the locals, who happily sit down to lengthy dinners where the accompanying wine and conversation flow in equal measure.

The province's cosmopolitan Montréal has long claimed to be the nation's fine-dining capital, but there's an appreciation of food here at all levels that also includes hearty pea soups, exquisite cheeses and tasty pâtés sold at bustling markets. In addition, there's also that national dish, poutine, waiting to clog your arteries, plus smoked-meat deli sandwiches.

Ontario – especially Toronto – is a microcosm of Canada's melting pot of cuisines. Like Québec, maple syrup is a super-sweet flavoring of choice here, and it's found in decadent desserts such as beavertails (fried, sugared dough) and on breakfast pancakes the size of Frisbees. Head south to the Niagara Peninsula wine region and you'll also discover restaurants

Eating Price Ranges

The following price ranges are for
main dishes:

$ less than $15

$$ $15–25

$$$ more than $25

fusing contemporary approaches and
traditional local ingredients, such as fish
from the Great Lakes.

Nunavut in the Arctic Circle is Canada's
newest territory, but it has a long history
of Inuit food, offering a real culinary adventure. Served in some restaurants (but
more often in family homes – make friends
with locals and they may invite you in for a
feast), regional specialties include boiled
seal and raw frozen char. You may also
encounter *maktaaq* – whale skin cut into
small pieces and swallowed whole.

In contrast, the central provinces of
Manitoba, Saskatchewan and Alberta have
their own deep-seated culinary ways. The
latter, Canada's cowboy country, is the
nation's beef capital – you'll find top-notch
Alberta steak on menus at leading restaurants across the country. If you're offered
'prairie oysters' here, though, you might
want to know (or maybe you'd prefer not
to!) that they're bull's testicles, prepared
in a variety of ways designed to take your
mind off their origin. In the Rockies things
get wilder – try elk, bison and even moose.

There's an old Eastern European influence over the border in Manitoba, where
immigrant Ukrainians have added comfort
food staples such as pierogi and thick, spicy
sausages. Head next door to prairie-land
Saskatchewan for dessert. The province's
heaping fruit pies are its most striking culinary contribution, especially when prepared
with tart Saskatoon berries.

In the far west, British Columbians have
traditionally fed themselves from the sea
and the fertile farmlands of the interior.
Okanagan Valley peaches, cherries and
blueberries – best purchased from seasonal roadside stands throughout the region
– are the staple of many summer diets.
But it's the seafood that attracts the lion's
share of culinary fans. Tuck into succulent
wild salmon, juicy Fanny Bay oysters and
velvet-soft scallops and you may decide
you've stumbled on foodie nirvana. There's
also a large and ever-growing influence of
Asian food in BC's Lower Mainland.

INTERNET ACCESS

➜ It's easy to find internet access. Libraries
and community agencies in practically every
town provide free wi-fi and computers for
public use. The only downsides are that usage
time is limited (usually 30 minutes), and some
facilities have erratic hours.

➜ Internet cafes are scarce, limited to the main
tourist areas in only certain towns; access
generally starts around $2 per hour.

➜ Wi-fi is widely available. Most lodgings have it
(in-room, with good speed), as do many restaurants, bars and Tim Hortons coffee shops.

LGBTIQ+ TRAVELERS

LGBTIQ+ travelers wil find Canada a
welcoming place to visit, although rural
areas are likely to be more conservative
than the big cities. Same-sex marriage is
legal throughout the country (Canada was
the fourth country in the world to legalize
same-sex marriage, in 2005).

Montréal, Toronto and Vancouver are
by far Canada's gayest cities, each with a
humming nightlife scene, publications and
lots of associations and support groups. All
have sizable Pride celebrations, too, which
attract big crowds.

Attitudes remain more conservative in
the northern regions. Throughout Nunavut, and to a lesser extent the Northwest
Territories, there are some retrogressive
attitudes toward homosexuality. The Yukon, in contrast, is more like British Columbia with a live-and-let-live West Coast
attitude.

The following are good resources for
LGBTIQ+ travel; they include Canadian
information, though not all are exclusive to
the region:

Damron (www.damron.com) Publishes several travel guides; gay-friendly tour operators
are listed on the website, too.

Out Traveler (www.outtraveler.com) Gay
travel magazine.

Purple Roofs (www.purpleroofs.com)
Website listing queer accommodations, travel
agencies and tours worldwide.

Queer Events (www.queerevents.ca) A
general resource for finding events that are
aimed at the gay community.

Xtra (www.xtra.ca) Source for gay and lesbian
news nationwide.

MONEY

➡ All prices quoted are in Canadian dollars ($), unless stated otherwise.

➡ Canadian coins come in 5¢ (nickel), 10¢ (dime), 25¢ (quarter), $1 (loonie) and $2 (toonie or twoonie) denominations. The gold-colored loonie features the loon, a common Canadian waterbird, while the two-toned toonie is decorated with a polar bear. Canada phased out its 1¢ (penny) coin in 2012.

➡ Paper currency comes in $5 (blue), $10 (purple), $20 (green) and $50 (red) denominations. The $100 (brown) and larger bills are less common. The newest bills in circulation – which have enhanced security features – are actually a polymer-based material; they feel more like plastic than paper.

➡ For changing money in the larger cities, currency exchange offices may offer better conditions than banks.

ATMs

➡ Many grocery and convenience stores, airports and bus, train and ferry stations have ATMs. Most are linked to international networks, the most common being Cirrus, Plus, Star and Maestro.

➡ Most ATMs also spit out cash if you use a major credit card. This method tends to be more expensive because, in addition to a service fee, you'll be charged interest immediately (in other words, there's no interest-free period as with purchases). For exact fees, check with your own bank or credit card company.

➡ Visitors heading to Canada's truly remote regions won't find an abundance of ATMs, so it is wise to cash up beforehand.

➡ Scotiabank, common throughout Canada, is part of the Global ATM Alliance. If your home bank is a member, fees may be less if you withdraw from Scotiabank ATMs.

Cash

Most Canadians don't carry large amounts of cash for everyday use, relying instead on credit and debit cards. Still, carrying some cash, say $100 or less, comes in handy when making small purchases. In some cases, cash is necessary to pay for rural B&Bs and shuttle vans; inquire in advance to avoid surprises. Shops and businesses rarely accept personal checks.

Credit Cards

Major credit cards such as MasterCard, Visa and American Express are widely accepted in Canada, except in remote, rural communities, where cash is king. You'll find it difficult or impossible to rent a car, book a room or order tickets over the phone without having a piece of plastic. Note that some credit card companies charge a 'transaction fee' (around 3% of whatever you purchased); check with your provider to avoid surprises.

If you are given an option to pay in your home country's currency, it is usually better to not accept, as they charge a higher interest rate for the point-of-sale transaction.

For lost or stolen cards, these numbers operate 24 hours:

American Express (☎800-869-3016; www.americanexpress.com)

MasterCard (☎800-307-7309; www.mastercard.com)

Visa (☎416-367-8472; www.visa.com)

Tipping

Tipping is a standard practice. Generally you can expect to tip for the following:

Restaurant waitstaff 15% to 20%

Bar staff $1 per drink

Hotel bellhop $1 to $2 per bag

Hotel room cleaners From $2 per day (depending on room size and messiness)

Taxis 10% to 15%

OPENING HOURS

Opening hours vary throughout the year. We've provided high-season opening hours; hours will generally decrease in the shoulder and low seasons.

Banks 10am–5pm Monday to Friday; some open 9am–noon Saturday

Restaurants breakfast 8–11am, lunch 11:30am–2:30pm Monday to Friday, dinner 5–9:30pm daily; some open for brunch 8am to 1pm Saturday and Sunday

Bars 5pm–2am daily

Clubs 9pm–2am Wednesday to Saturday

Shops 10am–6pm Monday to Saturday, noon–5pm Sunday; some open to 8pm or 9pm Thursday and/or Friday

Supermarkets 9am–8pm; some open 24 hours

PUBLIC HOLIDAYS

Canada observes 10 national public holidays and more at the provincial level. Banks, schools and government offices close on these days.

SAFE TRAVEL

Canada is one of the safest countries in the world. Pickpocketing and muggings are rare, especially if you take commonsense precautions. Panhandling is common, but usually not dangerous or aggressive.

➡ Stay in your car at all times when photographing wildlife.

➡ Drink spiking is rare but solo travelers should be cautious.

➡ With the exception of cannabis, recreational drug use in Canada is illegal, including magic mushrooms, and police can stop you any time you're behind the wheel.

➡ Forest fires, though rare, are a possible threat and should be treated seriously.

TELEPHONE

Canada's phone system is extensive and landlines reach most places; however, cell service can be spotty. Truly remote areas may not have any phone service at all.

Cell Phones

➡ If you have an unlocked GSM phone, you should be able to buy a SIM card from local providers such as **Telus** (www.telus.com), **Rogers** (www.rogers.com) or **Bell** (www.bell.ca). Bell has the best data coverage.

➡ US residents can often upgrade their domestic cell phone plan to extend to Canada. **Verizon** (www.verizonwireless.com) provides good results.

➡ Reception is poor and often nonexistent in rural areas no matter who your service provider is. Some companies' plans do not reach all parts of Canada, so check coverage maps.

➡ SIM cards that work for a set period, such seven, 14, 20 or 30 days, can be purchased online, often with United States and Canada voice, SMS and data bundled together.

Domestic & International Dialing

➡ Canadian phone numbers consist of a three-digit area code followed by a seven-digit local number. In many parts of Canada, you must dial all 10 digits preceded by 1, even if you're calling across the street. In other parts of the country, when you're calling within the same area code, you can dial the seven-digit number only, but this is slowly changing.

➡ For direct international calls, dial ☑011 + country code + area code + local phone number. The country code for Canada is 1 (same as for the USA, although international rates still apply for all calls made between the two countries).

➡ Toll-free numbers begin with ☑800, 877, 866, 855, 844 or 833 and must be preceded by 1. Some of these numbers are good throughout Canada and the USA, others only work within Canada, and some work in just one province.

TOURIST INFORMATION

➡ The **Canadian Tourism Commission** (www.canada.travel) is loaded with general information, packages and links.

➡ All provincial tourist offices maintain comprehensive websites packed with information helpful in planning your trip. Staff also field telephone inquiries and, on request, will mail out free maps and directories about accommodations, attractions and events.

VISAS

Currently, visas are not required for citizens of 46 countries – including the US, the UK, most EU members, Australia and New Zealand – for visits of up to six months.

Most arrivals from outside North America will need to complete an eTA. Information on eTAs and visas can be found at www.cic.gc.ca/english/visit/visas.asp.

Visitor visas – aka Temporary Resident Visas (TRVs) – can now be applied for online at www.cic.gc.ca/english/information/applications/visa.asp. Single-entry TRVs ($100) are usually valid for a maximum stay of six months from the date of your arrival in Canada. In most cases your biometric data (such as fingerprints) will be taken. Note that you don't need a Canadian multiple-entry TRV for repeated entries into Canada from the USA, unless you have visited a third country.

A separate visa is required for all nationalities if you plan to study or work in Canada.

Visa extensions ($100) need to be filed at least one month before your current visa expires (www.canada.ca/en/immigration-refugees-citizenship/services/visit-canada/extend-stay.html).

BEHIND THE SCENES

SEND US YOUR FEEDBACK

We love to hear from travelers – your comments help make our books better. We read every word, and we guarantee that your feedback goes straight to the authors. Visit **lonelyplanet. com/contact** to submit your updates and suggestions.

Note: We may edit, reproduce and incorporate your comments in Lonely Planet products such as guidebooks, websites and digital products, so let us know if you are happy to have your name acknowledged. For a copy of our privacy policy visit **lonelyplanet.com/legal**.

ACKNOWLEDGMENTS

Climate map data adapted from Peel MC, Finlayson BL & McMahon TA (2007) 'Updated World Map of the Köppen-Geiger Climate Classification', *Hydrology and Earth System Sciences*, 11, 1633–44.

Cover photograph: Horseshoe Falls, Niagara Peninsula, Ontario; Nagel Photography/Shutterstock©

THIS BOOK

This 1st edition of *Best Road Trips Ontario & Québec* was researched and written by Shawn Duthie, Steve Fallon, Carolyn Heller, Liza Prado and Phillip Tang. This guidebook was produced by the following:

Destination Editor Ben Buckner

Senior Product Editors Grace Dobell, Martine Power, Angela Tinson, Saralinda Turner

Product Editors Hannah Cartmel, Pete Cruttenden, Jenna Myers

Regional Senior Cartographer Corey Hutchison

Cartographer Julie Sheridan

Book Designers Catalina Aragón, Gwen Cotter, Aomi Ito

Assisting Editors Nigel Chin, James Smart

Cover Researcher Fergal Condon

Thanks to Hannah Cartmel, Joel Cotterell, Sonia Kapoor, Catherine Naghten

OUR STORY

A beat-up old car, a few dollars in the pocket and a sense of adventure. In 1972 that's all Tony and Maureen Wheeler needed for the trip of a lifetime – across Europe and Asia overland to Australia. It took several months, and at the end – broke but inspired – they sat at their kitchen table writing and stapling together their first travel guide, *Across Asia on the Cheap*. Within a week they'd sold 1500 copies. Lonely Planet was born.

Today, Lonely Planet has offices in the US, Ireland and China, with a network of more than 2000 contributors in every corner of the globe. We share Tony's belief that 'a great guidebook should do three things: inform, educate and amuse'.

INDEX

000 Map pages

000 Map pages

OUR WRITERS

SHAWN DUTHIE

Originally from Canada, Shawn has been traveling, studying and working around the world for the past 13 years. A love of travel merged with an interest in international politics, which led to several years of lecturing at the University of Cape Town and, now, as a freelance political risk consultant specialising in African countries. Shawn lives in South Africa and takes any excuse to travel around this amazing continent.

STEVE FALLON

A native of Boston, MA, Steve graduated from Georgetown University with a Bachelor of Science in modern languages. After working for several years for an American daily newspaper and earning a Master's degree in journalism, his fascination with the 'new' Asia led him to Hong Kong, where he lived for over a dozen years, working for a variety of media and running his own travel bookshop. He has written or contributed to more than 100 Lonely Planet titles.

CAROLYN HELLER

Carolyn has been a full-time travel, food, and feature writer since 1996, writing for publications including LonelyPlanet.com, *Forbes Travel Guide*, *Boston Globe*, *Los Angeles Times* and *Viator Travel*. The author of several guidebooks, she's also contributed to 50+ travel and restaurant guides for Lonely Planet and other publishers. She's eaten her way across more than 40 countries on six continents.

LIZA PRADO

Liza has been a travel writer since 2003, when she made a move from corporate lawyering to travel writing (and never looked back). She's written dozens of guidebooks and articles as well as apps and blogs to destinations across the Americas. She takes decent photos too. Liza is a graduate of Brown University and Stanford Law School. She lives very happily in Denver, Colorado, with her husband and fellow LP writer, Gary Chandler, and their two kids.

PHILLIP TANG

Phillip grew up on a typically Australian diet of pho and fish'n'chips before moving to Mexico City. A degree in Chinese- and Latin-American cultures launched him into travel and then writing about it for Lonely Planet's *Canada*, *China*, *Japan*, *Korea*, *Mexico*, *Peru* and *Vietnam* guides. Writing at hellophillip.com, photos @mrtangtangtang, and tweets @philliptang.

Published by Lonely Planet Global Limited
CRN 554153
1st edition – Oct 2022
ISBN 978 1 83869 567 5
© Lonely Planet 2022   Photographs © as indicated 2022
10 9 8 7 6 5 4 3 2 1
Printed in China

Although the authors and Lonely Planet have taken all reasonable care in preparing this book, we make no warranty about the accuracy or completeness of its content and, to the maximum extent permitted, disclaim all liability arising from its use.